Duck & Waffle

Duck & Waffle

Recipes and Stories

DANIEL DOHERTY

Photography by Anders Schønnemann

MITCHELL BEAZLEY

From a Crocodile to a Monkey

An Hachette UK Company
www.hachette.co.uk

First published in Great Britain in 2014
by Mitchell Beazley, a division of Octopus
Publishing Group Ltd,
Endeavour House, 189 Shaftesbury Avenue,
London WC2H 8JY
www.octopusbooks.co.uk

ISBN 978 1 84533 941 8

A CIP catalogue record for this book is available
from the British Library.

Printed and bound in China

10 9 8 7 6 5 4 3 2 1

Publisher Alison Starling
Senior Editor Sybella Stephens
Senior Art Editor Juliette Norsworthy
Home Economy & Food Styling Annie Rigg
Prop Styling Liz Belton
Senior Production Manager Katherine Hockley

Contents

The Duck & Waffle Story

To understand the Duck & Waffle story, you need to first understand a little bit about the man behind the brand: Shimon Bokovza. Shimon and his partners, Danielle Billera and Matthew Johnson, are the creators of Samba Brands Management, the restaurant management company of Duck & Waffle, Sushi Samba, Sugarcane Raw Bar Grill and Bocce Bar. Shimon is the kind of man who only accepts yes for an answer,

and in doing so, he does the impossible. He is a trendsetter, innovator and creative pioneer. For example, he opened Israel's first and only ski resort in 1969 at the tender age of 21. At that time it was new and fresh, and I bet many people told him he was crazy (which he is), but some things he just knows. He knows when to take a risk and follow his heart. He's a true visionary.

I had the pleasure of meeting Shimon at my previous job in Greenwich, where he instantaneously mesmerized me. While he often looked tired from travelling, the man was intense, driven and never missed a beat. I find it very difficult to write about him, as even now I still don't fully understand him. He has the attributes of a wonderful father, evident in the way he mentors people, from his ability to recognize and shape raw talent to his sheer honesty as he guides his team to meet expectations they would otherwise never attempt. He is quite simply one of the greatest individuals I have had the pleasure of working with. When someone like that is leading your team, anything is possible. You get the confidence to try new things and the thought of failure doesn't provoke fear. I can honestly say, with my hand on my heart, that I never want to work for anyone else.

It's hard to imagine that only two years ago I was trying to explain to my wife why I had accepted a job from a guy I barely knew, at a restaurant with no name, and with a first assignment to fly to Miami for two months to develop menus. I'm not usually that type of guy, I like my life

to be methodical, but I had such a great feeling about this endeavour because of Shimon's confidence and charisma. Sure enough, two weeks into my visit to Miami he was telling me that the restaurant would be called Duck & Waffle and would operate 24/7 in a part of London infamous for being dead at weekends. I thought he must be nuts – but he was right. We were, and have been, full from the beginning: 6 a.m. to 3 a.m. most nights, and all the way through on others. The name is cool, and the philosophy behind the restaurant is wonderful.

I spent almost two months in Miami working with Timon Balloo, Executive Chef of Sugarcane Raw Bar Grill. He's one of the most naturally talented chefs I have met and had the pleasure of cooking with. At the time, Sugarcane was Samba Brands Management's only non-Sushi Samba restaurant, and it has received great critical acclaim since opening in January 2010. I'd have taken any job in Timon's kitchen if I hadn't been due to open the restaurant in London. We cooked together, got to know each other and tried to figure

out how we could transfer the success of Sugarcane to London. Luckily, we had a very similar outlook on food, so that part was easy. The menu was super-seasonal, based on the simple components of sweet contrasted with salty, savoury and sour textures. It sounds fairly straightforward, but nobody understands this better than Timon.

Upon seeing the magnitude of the space in Heron Tower, Shimon decided to open two restaurants instead of just Sushi Samba. The 40th floor would be the home of another concept, whether inspired by Sugarcane or something else entirely. Sounds like a challenge, right? But that wasn't daunting enough for Shimon. Prior to Duck & Waffle, there was only one other 24-hour restaurant in London, so logically it would be yours truly who was tasked with creating another...on top of a skyscraper with crispy duck and waffles, but alas, I believed in it.

It was Danielle, the aforementioned managing partner and wife of Shimon – the sanity of the company – with her cool reason and calm intelligence, who suggested naming the restaurant after Timon's best-selling dish on the Sugarcane menu: duck and waffle. And what an idea that was! It has had a significant impact on London's culinary scene.

Today, Shimon is as present as ever – be it on the phone or stomping around the kitchen stealing nuts, he still tells me whether a dish is great, good or sucks. He pulls no punches and is straight to the point. We continue to better ourselves, to evolve and to build on what we have from within, using the great talents of the team. We are very lucky to have so many people, staff and guests, who believe in us, and in what we are trying to accomplish.

Of course, like any chef I have targets to hit and costs to monitor, but my sole calling is to cook and create, and that's the best feeling a chef can have. This book is not only a window into what we do at Duck & Waffle, but also a testament to each and every member of our team who has made the seemingly impossible possible, and that includes our wonderful guests, too.

I can't wait to see you in the clouds!

Daniel Doherty's Food Philosophy

Often people ask me what type of restaurant we are and what kind of food we do. The truth is I don't really know, and I don't think I ever will. I don't think that's necessarily a bad thing – we just cook seasonal food in a style that we think suits it best. Even though the menu includes many different cultures, we never mix them on the plate. The best phrase I could think of when asked by a journalist was 'often traditional, sometimes playful', which I think is fairly accurate. It's what best describes my cooking style and me. Whole roast Sunday chicken versus spicy ox cheek doughnut, baozi with bacon jam versus pea and ham soup. It's all about balance – I think you need some playfulness in life, but too much and it's overkill. As long as you take beautiful produce, at its peak, and cook it with love, you really can't go wrong.

When it comes to ingredients, I feel you must start with the basics. Good salt, extra virgin olive oil, real bread, natural vegetables, well-reared meat and fresh fish. If you don't start with those, you really have nothing. Seeing the love and passion that goes into making olive oil, the rigorous tastings, the variation from each country, region, producer and olive, is fascinating, and is reflected in all kinds of food production. Lord Newborough at Rhug Estate is a wonderful man, a man who doesn't compromise the quality of his organic meat, no matter the financial strain, and there are growers all over the country who feel the same about their beetroots or their carrots, bakers driving themselves crazy over making the perfect bread, and so on. If food doesn't make you excited in its rustic form, forget about refining it.

As the great Fergus Henderson says, 'Don't be afraid of your ingredients or they will misbehave.' He also said, 'Britain is blessed with short, wonderful seasons. Just pay attention and nature will write a menu for you.'

More important than any of the above is that you enjoy eating. One of my favourite things to do at work is to watch our guests from the open kitchen, and see their expressions. There is nothing more satisfying than seeing someone have a 'moment' when eating your food. As American writer Harriet van Horne once said, 'Cooking is like love, it should be entered into with abandon, or not at all'.

BREAKFAST AND BRUNCH

This is a healthy start to the day. The granola can be batch-made and kept in your bread bin, and the compote can be batch-made and frozen in smaller portions. This is what we eat at the restaurant most days, as one simply can't eat duck eggs baked in cream every day...although we do sometimes slip off the wagon.

Greek Yoghurt with Homemade Granola and Fruit Compote

Serves: 2

Preparation time: 15 minutes (if the granola is ready-made), plus cooling

Cooking time: 20 minutes

240g organic Greek yoghurt

4 tablespoons Granola (see page 218)

4 tablespoons Fruit Compote (see below) or fresh fruit

For the fruit compote

600g mixed summer berries

50g caster sugar

1 star anise

juice of 1 orange

To make the compote, put the fruit into a saucepan with the sugar, star anise and orange juice. Place over a medium heat, bring to the boil, then lower the heat and simmer for approximately 20 minutes, or until the liquid has reduced and you are left with a thick mixture. Allow to cool, then refrigerate until you are ready to use. Any leftover can either be frozen, or stored in a plastic container in the fridge for up to 1 week.

To serve, simply layer the yoghurt, granola and compote in a bowl and enjoy!

Having a free-flowing supply of waffles meant we just had to offer a sweet version. This is one of our most successful combinations. Others that have worked really well are summer berries with Chantilly cream, and caramelized apples, toffee sauce and cinnamon ice cream. The variations are endless, so be creative and adventurous. I recommend making the chocolate hazelnut spread instead of buying it – it lasts for ages if stored in the fridge, and is worth the effort!

Sweet Belgian Waffles

Serves: 2
Preparation time: 45 minutes
Cooking time: 15 minutes

oil, for brushing
half batch of Waffle Mix
(see page 140)
2 bananas
caster sugar, for dusting
2 scoops of Vanilla Ice Cream
(see page 219)

For the chocolate hazelnut spread

50g hazelnuts
60g icing sugar
10g cocoa powder
25g drinking chocolate
50g plain chocolate
(65% cocoa solids), melted
1 tablespoon rapeseed oil
75ml water

For the peanut crunch
100g caster sugar
a splash of water
50g peanuts

You will also need a waffle iron

To make the chocolate hazelnut spread, preheat your oven to 180°C/gas mark 4. Put the hazelnuts on a baking tray and roast until golden (approximately 5 minutes). Place in a food processor and blend until ground. Add the icing sugar, cocoa powder and drinking chocolate and blend together, then add the melted chocolate and blend for about 5 minutes. Gradually add the oil and water.

To make the peanut crunch, put the sugar and water into a saucepan over a medium heat and cook until it becomes a caramel. Add the peanuts and mix well, then turn out on to a baking sheet lined with baking paper. Allow to set, then smash with the end of a rolling pin into small pieces.

When ready to serve, turn on your waffle iron and cook the waffles: Brush the hot waffle iron with oil and pour a ladle of batter into each mould. Spread it all around, as the mix is quite thick and won't spread on its own. Cook until golden and cooked through, about 3 minutes.

Split the bananas in half lengthways, dust with a couple of pinches of caster sugar and caramelize with a blowtorch.

To serve, build up each dish with a waffle on the bottom, then a good spoonful of hazelnut spread, then the bananas and the ice cream. Finally, sprinkle with the peanut crunch.

We created the Dossant after being inspired by New York's Cronut, which was dreamed up by Dominique Ansell, who started a craze with the first croissant/doughnut hybrid. Instead of making a doughnut-shaped croissant, we cook and fill a croissant like a doughnut. You can play around with the flavours as you get more confident with making the crème pâtissière. You can also try making the croissants from scratch, but it's quite tricky, and using frozen ones is fine.

Dossants with Coffee and Amaretto

Makes: 8

Preparation time: 2 hours

Cooking time: 30 minutes

vegetable oil, for deep-frying

8 croissants (frozen is fine, but they must be uncooked)

100g caster sugar, for rolling

nibbed or flaked almonds, toasted, to garnish

For the crème pâtissière

250ml milk

400ml double cream

1 vanilla pod, seeds only

1 egg

3 egg yolks

50g cornflour

125g caster sugar

1 double espresso

25ml Amaretto liqueur

For the almond crunch

100g caster sugar

2 tablespoons water

50g flaked almonds

You will also need a deep-fat fryer and a piping bag

The crème pâtissière should be made in advance, as it needs time to cool. Put the milk, cream and vanilla seeds into a saucepan and heat to just before boiling point. Meanwhile, mix the egg, egg yolks, cornflour and sugar in a bowl. When the milk and cream mix is hot, pour it slowly into the bowl of eggs, while whisking. Return the mixture to the pan and lower the heat. Continue to stir until it thickens to a mayonnaise-like consistency, taking care that it doesn't catch on the bottom of the pan or scramble.

Pass the mixture through a sieve, using a dough scraper to push it through, which will result in a thick silky custard. Put a layer of clingfilm directly on top so a skin doesn't form, and set aside to cool.

Next, make the almond crunch. Put the sugar and water into a saucepan over a medium heat and cook until it becomes a caramel. Add the nuts and mix well, then turn out on to a baking sheet lined with baking paper and leave to cool. When cool it will be hard, so smash it into pieces with a rolling pin. Store in a dry place, but not in the fridge.

When ready to cook and serve, heat the oil to 160°C in your deep-fat fryer and drop in your frozen croissants. How long you cook them for will depend on their size – a normal croissant will take about 20 minutes, turning every 4–5 minutes, and a mini one (about a third of the size) will take 10 minutes.

While the croissants are cooking, add the coffee and Amaretto to the crème pâtissière and whisk well. Spoon into a piping bag.

When the croissants are ready, take them out of the fryer and let them drain on kitchen paper. Roll them in the caster sugar, then make a cut all the way down one side. Pipe in the crème pâtissière and sprinkle with the almond crunch and the toasted almonds. Eat immediately for maximum effect.

This is a recipe I picked up in Miami, and it's now our top-selling breakfast dish. Back in March 2012, when I was working at our sister restaurant Sugarcane, in Midtown Miami, one of the Colombian chefs was making breakfast to aid his tender feeling after quite a heavy night. He told us about a dish called 'perico', based on scrambled eggs, spring onions and tomatoes, which he loves to eat when hungover. I loved the lightness of it – in the UK we tend to go heavy when in need of some TLC, but this was light, and vegetarian. I added some ripe avocado and put the whole thing on toast, and a winner was born. At the restaurant we offer grilled chorizo sausage or smoked salmon as an add-on.

Colombian Eggs

Serves: 2

Preparation time: 10 minutes

Cooking time: 5 minutes

20g unsalted butter

2 spring onions, finely sliced on the angle

4 eggs, beaten

1 plum tomato, quartered, deseeded and cut into 1cm dice

sea salt and freshly ground black pepper

2 slices of sourdough bread

1 ripe avocado, cut into 5mm thick slices

Melt the butter in a frying pan. When it's foaming, add the spring onions and cook until soft, taking care not to let them burn.

Add the eggs and scramble lightly. Finish with the diced tomatoes and season with salt and pepper.

Toast the sourdough and lay the avocado on top. Spoon the eggs over, season again and serve.

Pearl barley is a great ingredient, and one that we use a lot in the restaurant. It's super-healthy, and can be used in many ways. This is one of our signature dishes, and I've also given a variation that I sometimes eat for lunch.

Pearl Barley Ragout with Goat's Curd and a Fried Egg

Serves: 4

Preparation time: 20 minutes, plus soaking

Cooking time: 1 hour

50ml olive oil, plus extra for frying the eggs

2 onions, finely chopped

2 garlic cloves, finely chopped

1 bay leaf

1 sprig of fresh thyme

200g pearl barley, soaked overnight in cold water

300ml vegetable stock or Chicken Stock (see page 216)

30g unsalted butter, plus extra for frying the eggs

2 handfuls of mixed wild mushrooms

sea salt and freshly ground black pepper

30g Confit Shallots (see page 217)

4 eggs

2 sprigs of fresh parsley, chopped

2 sprigs of fresh coriander, chopped

4 tablespoons goat's curd

Balsamic Glaze (see page 217), to finish (optional)

First you need to cook the barley. Once cooked, it can stay in the fridge for up to 3 days.

Heat the 50ml oil in a large saucepan, add the onions, garlic, bay leaf and thyme, and cook gently for 5–10 minutes, until they start to soften. Drain the soaked barley and add to the pan. Mix well and slowly add the stock, as if you were making a risotto. Once all the stock is used and absorbed, pour the barley on to a baking tray lined with baking paper, removing the thyme and bay leaf, and leave to cool. At this point you can refrigerate the barley and save it for later.

When ready to eat, heat a frying pan and add the butter. When it's foaming, add the mushrooms and sauté for 3–4 minutes. Season with salt and pepper, then add the barley and give it a good shake in the pan. Continue to sauté for 5 minutes. Add the confit shallots and correct the seasoning.

At this point, heat a drizzle of olive oil in a large frying pan, and when hot, add a knob of butter. When it begins to foam, add the eggs, season with salt and pepper, and gently fry for 2–3 minutes. If you like them well done, flip over to seal the tops.

Finish the barley ragout with the parsley and coriander. Place 1 tablespoon of goat's curd on each serving plate, and spread it out. Divide the barley between the plates, and top each one with a fried egg. Finish each plate with a little balsamic glaze (see page 217) if you like.

VARIATION

Try swapping the wild mushrooms and goat's curd for Peperonata (see page 59) and chorizo. Peel away the skin from 3 cooking chorizo sausages and dice them into 1cm cubes. Sauté for a couple of minutes so that the natural oils come out, then add the barley, and after cooking together for 3–4 minutes, fold through the peperonata and finish with an egg.

This is one of our most luxurious breakfast dishes, perfect at the end of a hard night or as a treat on a Sunday morning. You can play about with the ingredients you use – a layer of spinach at the bottom of the dish is a good addition, as is diced smoked haddock in place of the mushrooms. It also makes a nice starter.

Duck Egg en Cocotte with Wild Mushrooms and Gruyère Cheese

Serves: 2
Preparation time: 10 minutes
Cooking time: 30 minutes

butter, for greasing

1 tablespoon olive oil

2 shallots, finely chopped

1 sprig of fresh thyme

½ a garlic clove

1 bay leaf

1 handful of wild mushrooms, roughly chopped into 2cm pieces

½ a glass of white wine

150ml double cream

sea salt and freshly ground black pepper

2 duck eggs

2 slices of sourdough bread

20g Gruyère cheese, grated

3–5 truffle slices per person

Butter the insides of two 100ml ramekins or individual cocottes.

Heat the olive oil in a saucepan and cook the shallots with the thyme, garlic and bay leaf until softened. Add the mushrooms and cook for 5 minutes more, then add the wine and simmer until reduced by three-quarters. Add the cream and continue to cook until reduced by half, then season with salt and pepper.

When ready to serve, preheat your oven to 180°C/gas mark 4.

Place half the sauce in the bottom of each ramekin, removing the thyme and bay leaf, then crack a duck egg into each. Top with the rest of the sauce, and place in the oven for 3 minutes.

Toast the bread and cut into soldiers. When the 3 minutes is up, or the whites have started to form, add the cheese to the ramekins and cook for a further 4–8 minutes, depending on how you like your eggs cooked.

Garnish with the truffle slices and eat straight away with the toasted soldiers.

Smoked haddock and English mustard go really well together, and are both wonderful British ingredients. The inspiration came from the dish Omelette Arnold Bennett, named after a writer who requested smoked haddock omelette with Gruyère every time he stayed at the Savoy hotel in the late 1890s.

Smoked Haddock with Hash Browns and English Mustard Cream

Serves: 2

Preparation time: 10 minutes

Cooking time: 30 minutes

400g smoked haddock, skinned (reserve the skin)

2 potatoes, skin left on, parboiled so they are 50% cooked

1 bunch of spring onions

sea salt and freshly ground black pepper

500ml milk

2 cloves

2 sprigs of fresh thyme

1 bay leaf

1 tablespoon olive oil

2 shallots, finely chopped

1 glass of white wine

200ml Chicken Stock (see page 216)

200ml double cream

1 tablespoon English mustard

a squeeze of lemon juice

vegetable oil, for shallow-frying

2 eggs

Cut the haddock into 2 portions and set aside.

Grate the potatoes and finely chop the spring onions. Mix together and season with salt and pepper. Shape into 4 hash browns, and set aside until ready to serve.

Put the milk, cloves, 1 sprig of thyme and the bay leaf into a medium saucepan and bring slowly to the boil. Add a pinch of salt, then lower the heat for 10 minutes to infuse the flavours into the milk. Strain into another saucepan and set aside.

To make the sauce, put the olive oil, shallots, the other sprig of thyme and the haddock skin into a saucepan and cook gently for 8–10 minutes, or until soft but with no colour. Add the wine and simmer until reduced by three-quarters, then add the chicken stock and continue to simmer until reduced by half. Add the cream, season with salt and pepper and bring to the boil, then lower the heat again and simmer until thick. Whisk in the mustard and lemon juice, then strain.

When ready to serve, warm the milk over a medium heat and drop in the haddock. After 6 minutes it should be cooked. Meanwhile, shallow-fry the hash browns in a little vegetable oil for 2–3 minutes each side, or until cooked, then poach your eggs.

Serve each piece of haddock with an egg on top, with 2–3 tablespoons of sauce spooned over, and the hash browns on the side.

In America this is called 'toad in the hole', and in New Zealand it's 'frog in the pond', but for obvious reasons we couldn't use the first name, and the latter didn't feel right, so we created our own name: 'egg in a basket'. This is my idea of a perfect brunch dish, and it's one I regularly cook at home too.

Duck Egg in a Brioche Basket

Serves: 2
Preparation time: 5 minutes
Cooking time: 10 minutes

2 tablespoons olive oil
2 slices of brioche, 2.5cm thick
2 duck eggs
40g Gruyère cheese, grated
20g butter
3–5 truffle slices per person
6 small fresh basil leaves
sea salt and freshly ground black pepper
1 handful of watercress
30ml Sherry Dressing (see page 215)

Preheat your oven to 160°C/gas mark 3.

Heat the olive oil in a large ovenproof frying pan over a medium heat. Using a biscuit cutter, cut a 5cm hole in the centre of each slice of brioche. Add the brioche to the pan, and crack a duck egg into the middle of each one. Allow the eggs to start cooking on the base.

As soon as the white starts to firm up, scatter the cheese all over both brioches and add the butter to the pan. Place in the oven for approximately 3–6 minutes, depending how you like your eggs – the cheese should be melted and the yolk should still be runny.

Garnish with the truffle slices and basil leaves, season with salt and pepper and serve with the watercress, drizzled with the sherry dressing, on the side.

As if this recipe isn't enough, we also have the Fat Boy variation, where we add maple-glazed bacon and a fried duck egg to the sandwich. Sounds weird, but trust me. Just make sure you have a lie down afterwards...

Toasted PBJ with Banana and Berries

Makes: 2
Preparation time: 10 minutes
Cooking time: 15 minutes

4 slices of brioche, 2cm thick
2 tablespoons strawberry jam
2 tablespoons peanut butter
2 bananas, sliced 5mm thick
60g unsalted butter
200ml double cream
40g caster sugar
seeds from ½ a vanilla pod
2 small handfuls of mixed seasonal berries
icing sugar, for dusting

Preheat your oven to 160°C/gas mark 3.

Spread 2 slices of brioche with the jam, and the other 2 with the peanut butter. Add the sliced banana to the jam slices and put the peanut butter slices on top, to make 2 sandwiches.

Heat an ovenproof frying pan and add half the butter. When it starts foaming, add the sandwiches and cook over a medium heat until golden brown. Turn them over and add the rest of the butter, then place the pan in the oven for approximately 10 minutes, or until golden on top and warm inside.

In the meantime, whip the cream, sugar and vanilla seeds to soft peak stage.

Take out the sandwiches, place on a chopping board and cut them in half. Serve with a dollop of whipped cream and the seasonal berries on top, and dusted with icing sugar.

Beans on toast is a British staple, and I felt obliged to reinvent it. When I was at school I had a part-time job in a restaurant in my home town, Shrewsbury, which became full-time during the holidays. On my split shifts, I'd pop home and, without fail, have two rounds of beans on toast with cheese on top. I'll never forget those moments between manic shifts where holding a knife was daunting, and I think about it every time we serve this dish.

Beans on Toast

Serves: 4–6

Preparation time: 20 minutes, plus cooling

Cooking time: 3½ hours

200g dried white beans, soaked overnight, or 500g ready-to-go cooked beans

300ml passata

1 onion, finely diced

2 garlic cloves, crushed

1 sprig of fresh thyme

1 sprig of fresh rosemary

1 bay leaf

1 smoked ham hock

300ml Chicken Stock (see page 216)

2 chipotles en adobo from a jar

50g demerara sugar

1 tablespoon paprika

sea salt and freshly ground black pepper

2 tablespoons Bacon Jam (see page 200)

100g Montgomery's or other good mature Cheddar cheese, grated

sourdough bread, toasted, to serve

Preheat your oven to 160°C/gas mark 3.

Place all the ingredients apart from the bacon jam, cheese and toast into an ovenproof casserole dish and cover with a lid. Place in the oven and leave for a good 3–3½ hours until the hock gives way under a gentle push with a fork. If using ready-to-go beans, add them an hour before the hock is ready.

When this stage is reached, remove from the oven, and allow to cool. Take out the ham hock and remove the skin, then shred the meat with your fingers and put it back into the casserole with the beans.

At this stage you can chill the dish, or bring it back up to temperature to serve. If serving now, turn on your grill. Heat up the bacon jam, and toast your bread.

When the beans are hot, transfer them to a baking dish and top with the cheese. Place under the grill to melt and brown.

To serve, spread the bacon jam on the toast, and add a good ladleful of beans on top.

Here's another dish that can soothe your pains, one which, with the addition of one or all of the three magical ingredients (bacon, cheese and hot sauce), can further aid your recovery. This is the kind of food we have found people tend to look for around the 4 a.m. mark, but it also works as a post-sleep cure.

Salt Beef Hash with Poached Egg and Hollandaise

Makes: 2 hangover-size portions
Preparation time: 45 minutes, plus cooling
Cooking time: 3 hours

olive oil

10 new potatoes, cooked and halved

sea salt and freshly ground black pepper

2 tablespoons Confit Shallots (see page 217)

2 eggs

2 pickled gherkins, sliced 5mm thick

For the beef

1 piece (approximately 500g) salt beef

1 onion, peeled and halved

1 bay leaf

1 carrot, peeled and split in half lengthways

For the hollandaise

30ml white wine

30ml white wine vinegar

2 peppercorns

1 sprig of fresh thyme

2 egg yolks

250g unsalted butter, clarified (heated so the fats and milks separate – discard the milks)

1 tablespoon English mustard

1 squeeze of lemon juice

Place the salt beef in a medium saucepan. Cover with cold water, and add the onion, bay leaf and carrot. Bring to the boil, then lower the heat to a simmer and cook for approximately 2½ hours, or until the beef gives when pushed with the back of a spoon. Allow to cool in the stock. When cool, cut into 5mm slices.

Preheat your oven to 180°C/gas mark 4, and bring a saucepan of water to the boil.

Heat a splash of olive oil in an ovenproof frying pan and add the potatoes and salt beef. Season with salt and pepper. Once sizzling, put the pan into the oven for about 10 minutes, or until the beef starts to become golden brown.

Next, make the hollandaise. Put the wine, vinegar, peppercorns and thyme into a small saucepan and bring to the boil. Reduce the heat and simmer until reduced by half, then strain into a bowl. Add the egg yolks, and whisk over a saucepan of simmering water until light and fluffy. This should take around 5 minutes. If the water starts to boil below the bowl, turn off the heat – there will be enough heat in the pan to cook the eggs, but just be careful they don't scramble.

Very slowly start adding the clarified butter while whisking constantly, until the mixture has a mayonnaise-like consistency. If it gets too thick, adding a teaspoon of warm water will bring it back to life. Stir in the mustard and lemon juice. The hollandaise will hold in a warm place for at least 30 minutes – next to your stove should be fine. Just be careful it's not too warm or it may split.

Remove the hash from the oven, and add the confit shallots. Give it a little sauté on the stove for a further 5 minutes.

At this point poach your eggs, keeping an eye on your hollandaise.

Turn the salt beef hash on to plates and add the pickled gherkins. Serve the poached eggs on top, season with pepper and give them a good coating of hollandaise.

A hash that involves potato, spicy pork and onions, topped with a runny egg and cheese, is my perfect hangover cure. I also like to add a few splashes of hot sauce at the end, to really blow out the toxins. You will need a sleep afterwards, it's part of the recipe after all...

Hangover Hash

Serves: 2

Preparation time: 20 minutes, plus cooling

Cooking time: 2 hours

Resting time: 1 hour's sleep

10 new potatoes

sea salt

1 x 12cm cooking chorizo sausage, cut into 1cm dice

olive oil

2 tablespoons Peperonata (see page 59)

2 eggs

100g Gruyère cheese, grated

sea salt and freshly ground black pepper

For the onion jam

50ml olive oil

2 large onions, finely sliced

1 bay leaf

First, make the onion jam. Heat the olive oil in a medium saucepan, then add the onions and bay leaf and cook gently until soft. Keep cooking them over a low heat for about an hour, or until they slowly start turning golden brown and the natural sugars start to caramelize. At this point you can chill the jam and keep it in the fridge (you could make a double batch and save half for future use).

Cook the potatoes in a saucepan of salted water for approximately 20 minutes. When ready, strain and allow to cool. Cut each one in half.

Preheat your oven to 180°C/gas mark 4.

Put the chorizo, potatoes and a drizzle of olive oil into an ovenproof frying pan and place in the oven for 10 minutes. Add the peperonata and onion jam and give it a mix. Return the pan to the oven for a further 10 minutes. Next, crack the eggs on top and cover with the cheese. Return the pan to the oven until the cheese is melted and the white of the egg is cooked, but the yolk is still runny – approximately 5–10 minutes, depending on how you like your eggs. Take out of the oven, season with salt and pepper and eat straight away, as the egg will continue to cook.

We serve fresh fish from
Cornwall & Scotland. Our
meats are from the RHUG
Estate, North Wales...

...and

www.facebook.com/duckandwaffle

Meatballs are one of the best comfort foods around. This recipe is one of my favourites – as the ricotta gets moved around the dish as you eat, the sauce becomes slightly enriched and creamy. Once you master meatballs, you'll have great fun playing with flavour combinations, changing the meats and spices, the sauces and the starch. Personally, I like a good scoop of mash with mine, but bread or pasta work just fine too. You can buy ricotta if you don't have time to make it.

Meatballs with Fennel and Ricotta

Serves: 4

Preparation time: 1 hour

Cooking time: 30 minutes

100g butter

50g fresh breadcrumbs

olive oil

1 head of fennel, sliced 1mm thick on a mandolin

2 tablespoons Onion Jam (see page 36)

500ml Chicken Stock (see page 216)

sea salt and freshly ground black pepper

50g Parmesan cheese, grated

2 tablespoons pine nuts, toasted

For the ricotta

2 litres whole milk

a pinch of sea salt

juice of 2 lemons

For the meatballs

500g minced pork

100g finocchiona salami, finely diced or minced

50g fresh breadcrumbs

1 egg

a pinch of fennel seeds

1 sprig of fresh rosemary, finely chopped

1 sprig of fresh oregano, finely chopped

First, make the ricotta. Heat the milk until just below boiling, then add the salt and the lemon juice and allow to sit, undisturbed, for 10 minutes. After this time, the milk should have curdled. Strain through a muslin cloth and allow to sit for a further 30 minutes. You can use it at this stage, or wrap it in the cloth and hang it in your fridge, above a bowl, for a drier ricotta.

Melt 50g butter in a frying pan over a medium heat and add the breadcrumbs. Toast until golden brown, stirring often. If they start to colour too quickly, lower the heat. Set aside and allow to cool.

To make the meatballs, combine all the ingredients together and mix well. Roll into golfball-size balls.

Preheat your oven to 180°C/gas mark 4.

Heat a drizzle of olive oil in a frying pan, then add the meatballs and fry them all over to seal. Put them into an ovenproof dish.

Put the shaved fennel into the same frying pan with 1 tablespoon olive oil and cook gently for approximately 10 minutes. Add the onion jam and the chicken stock, bring to the boil, then reduce the heat and simmer until reduced by three-quarters. Add the remaining butter and swirl it around so that it emulsifies and combines into a sauce, then season with salt and pepper. Pour the mix over the meatballs.

Place in the oven for 10 minutes, then remove, sprinkle with the Parmesan and spoon over a couple of tablespoons of ricotta. Put back into the oven for a further 5 minutes, or until the Parmesan has browned. Take out, sprinkle the reserved browned breadcrumbs and pine nuts evenly over the top and serve immediately.

Makes: 4

Preparation time: 30 minutes

Cooking time: 10–20 minutes, depending on how you want your burgers cooked

For the burger mix

1 onion, finely chopped

2 tablespoons vegetable oil

sea salt and freshly ground black pepper

300g short rib beef, minced

300g chuck steak, minced

1 gherkin, finely chopped

2 cloves of Confit Garlic (see page 217)

1 tablespoon Dijon mustard

2 splashes of Tabasco

For the special sauce

2 tablespoons Mayonnaise (see page 217)

1 tablespoon tomato ketchup

1 gherkin, finely chopped

1 shallot, finely chopped

1 teaspoon English mustard

2 sprigs of fresh dill, finely chopped

1 tablespoon Sriracha hot sauce

To assemble

4 slices Gruyère cheese

4 brioche buns

4 tablespoons Onion Jam (see page 36)

8 baby gem leaves

Leo Sayer – all dayer. Modern cockney rhyming slang. Zeren Wilson, of Bitten & Written, once did an all-nighter when we first opened, and it was when he said he was 'on a Leo' that the idea struck me. We wanted to create a burger that satisfied everyone's needs over a 24-hour period, and this is what we came up with. Needless to say, on request, eggs, bacon, avocado, hash browns and mushrooms have all been added (once all together in a single burger), so I'll leave the 'extras' to you.

Leo Sayer Burger

For the burger, first cook the onion gently in the oil for a few minutes without colouring. Tip the cooked onion into a large bowl, season with salt and pepper, combine with all the other burger ingredients and work together well. Divide into 4 and shape into patties.

For the special sauce, mix all the ingredients together in a bowl.

Cook the burgers on a griddle or, even better, on a barbecue, for 3 minutes on each side for medium rare, 4 minutes for medium and 6–8 minutes for well done.

Add the cheese on top and melt under a hot grill for 1 minute, then build up your buns with the special sauce, onion jam, gem leaves and whatever else takes your fancy.

There is no recipe as such for this; everyone has different 'needs' in their time of pain. The idea came from my time in Miami, when, on my second to last day, we all went out and got a little crazy, and to say I was feeling it the next day would be the understatement of the year. Eric, one of the managers, demanded I ate one of his hangover pizzas, and wouldn't take no for an answer. Knowing Eric well, most of the chefs knew exactly what it consisted of, and after a good 10 minutes of pushing through, my hangover was cured. Below is my medicine; yours will be different, no doubt.

Hangover Pizza

Serves: 1

Preparation time: 1½ hours

Cooking time: 12 minutes (maybe longer if you add more ingredients...)

For the dough

400g strong white flour

125g semolina flour

2 teaspoons sea salt

12g fresh yeast or 1 sachet of fast-acting instant yeast

300ml lukewarm water

50ml olive oil

2 tablespoons passata

4 rashers of streaky bacon, cooked

a small handful of grated Cheddar cheese

½ a ball of mozzarella cheese, torn into quarters

3 splashes of hot sauce

1 tablespoon Peperonata (see page 59)

1 tablespoon Onion Jam (see page 36)

1 egg

another handful of grated Cheddar

more bacon

more cheese

This is so wrong, my wife would kill me. But anyway, the cure begins...

To make the dough, sift the flours together and add the salt. Mix the yeast, water and oil together in a bowl. Make a well in the flour, and add the yeast liquid. Gradually work the flour and liquid together to form a dough. Continue to knead for 10 minutes, or until the dough is smooth and elastic. Set it aside to rest for 1 hour, or until doubled in size.

Preheat your oven to as hot as it will go and line a baking sheet with oiled baking paper.

On a floured surface, give the dough a quick knead to knock the air out of it. Roll the dough out nice and thin, aiming for 2mm, give or take, and place it on the prepared baking sheet.

Build up the toppings creating cheesy layers, and leaving the egg until last. If loading lots of ingredients, you may want to precook your base so it doesn't go soggy. Make sure you create a small dip in the centre so the egg doesn't roll out.

Bake for approximately 10–12 minutes, or until the dough is cooked and crisp. Note that this varies from oven to oven, so keep a close eye on it.

Another comfort food idea, this one is traditionally made with beef. You can omit the lamb's breast if you don't have time to cure and confit – it's just there for a nice crunch, which can also be achieved by crumbling some ready-salted crisps on top (sounds strange, but it works).

Smoky Mutton Sloppy Joe with Crispy Lamb's Breast

Makes: 6
Preparation time: 1 day
Cooking time: 4½ hours

For the lamb

100g piece of lamb's breast

100g Standard Cure (see page 218)

200g duck fat

vegetable oil, for frying

plain flour, for dusting

sea salt and freshly ground black pepper

For the sloppy Joe mix

500g minced mutton

2 onions, finely diced

2 garlic cloves, finely chopped

4 chipotles en adobo from a jar, mashed to a rough paste

2 teaspoons harissa

2 sprigs of fresh rosemary

4 bay leaves

40g tomato paste

200g tomato ketchup

60ml Worcestershire sauce

60ml soy sauce

To assemble

6 brioche hot dog buns

fresh coriander leaves, to garnish

The day before, sprinkle the lamb's breast all over with the cure. Put it into a container with a lid and leave in the fridge overnight.

The next day, preheat your oven to 130°C/gas mark ½. Take out the lamb's breast and brush off all of the cure. Place the lamb in an ovenproof dish, add the duck fat to cover, and confit for approximately 3 hours, or until the meat is tender and gives easily when pushed with a spoon. Allow to cool in the fat. When cool enough to handle, pull the meat into strands with your fingers, then store in the fridge.

To make the sloppy Joe mix, put the minced mutton into a frying pan over a medium heat, and pour away any fat as it melts. Add the onions and garlic and continue to cook for a further 10 minutes, or until the onions are soft. Add the remaining sloppy Joe ingredients and cook over a low heat for approximately 1 hour, like you would any ragout.

Heat the oil to 180°C in a deep-fat fryer or in a deep heavy-based saucepan. Dust a handful of the lamb's breast with flour and fry for 2–3 minutes, or until crisp. Place on kitchen paper to dry, and season with salt and pepper.

Flash the brioche buns in a warm oven or toast them lightly, and serve the sloppy Joe mix in the buns, the same way as you would a hot dog. Garnish with the crispy lamb breast and the coriander leaves.

Extreme gluttony alert! Another 4 a.m. before-you-go-to-sleep or 10 a.m. I-need-some-love dish. As always, feel free to add one of the magical three: bacon, more cheese or hot sauce.

Grilled Cheese Sandwich with Ox Cheek and Pickled Fennel

Serves: 2

Preparation time: 20 minutes (if you have ox cheek braised already), plus pickling time

Cooking time: 20–25 minutes

4 slices of sourdough bread

100g Braised Ox Cheek (see page 102)

4 slices Taleggio cheese, cut to the same size as your bread

50g unsalted butter

8 pieces of Pickled Fennel (see below)

2 tablespoons Hollandaise (see page 34)

For the pickled fennel

1 head of fennel

300ml Pickling Liquid (see page 216)

Slice the fennel 1mm thick and put it into a bowl. Pour over the pickling liquid to cover and leave for at least 3 hours.

Take 2 slices of bread and divide the ox cheek between them. Add 2 slices of cheese to each. Close the sandwich with the other 2 slices of bread.

Heat an ovenproof frying pan and preheat your oven to 180°C/gas mark 4.

Add half the butter to the frying pan. When it's foaming, add the sandwiches and cook until golden brown. Carefully turn them over and add the other half of the butter. Place in the oven until the cheese is melted, the ox cheek is hot and the bread is golden brown on the bottom. This should take around 10 minutes.

Remove from the oven and place each sandwich on a plate. Open them up and add 4 pieces of the pickled fennel and a tablespoon of hollandaise to each one. Close up the sandwiches and eat immediately.

SMALL PLATES

Using granola in a savoury salad adds a different texture and dimension. Try using different fruits and nuts to suit your fancy. Use Amalfi lemons if you can get them, because they are, simply put, the best lemons in the world. Natoora, who deliver in the UK through Ocado, have them readily available. If you can't find Amalfi lemons, any unwaxed lemon will do. Another good ingredient to have in your cupboard is balsamic glaze; at the restaurant we reduce aged balsamic vinegar to create a beautiful glaze that's both sweet and acidic, but this can be tricky to get right, and now you can buy it in most shops to save you the stress. If you fancy making your own, see page 217.

Smoked Ricotta with Granola and Candied Lemon

Serves: 4

Preparation time: 10 minutes (if you have the candied lemon, granola and balsamic glaze ready; 2 hours, plus drying time if not)

Assembly time: 20 minutes

10 fresh sage leaves

vegetable oil, for frying

100g watercress

150g Granola (see page 218)

100g smoked ricotta (or ricotta salata if you can't find smoked ricotta), shaved with a peeler

2 tablespoons Sherry Dressing (see page 216)

2 teaspoons Balsamic Glaze (see page 217)

2 teaspoons honey

3 teaspoons of Candied Lemon (see below)

For the candied lemon

2 Amalfi lemons

1 litre water

100g caster sugar

To make the candied lemon, peel the skin away from the lemons and trim off any white pith. Slice the skin into matchstick-size pieces. Bring 300ml of the water to the boil in a saucepan. Add the lemon, and leave for 10 seconds. Remove from the water and place in iced water to stop the cooking process. Repeat this process three times. This removes any bitterness from the lemon.

Put the sugar into a saucepan with the remaining 100ml of water and stir to dissolve. Bring to the boil, then add the blanched lemon peel and simmer for 5 minutes. Remove and spread out on a baking sheet lined with baking paper. Leave to dry for a few hours, or until crisp.

Meanwhile, fry the sage leaves in hot oil for 10 seconds, or until crisp, and drain on kitchen paper.

To make the salad, put the watercress, granola and ricotta into a bowl and dress with the sherry dressing. Arrange with plenty of height on a serving plate or in a bowl. Drizzle over the balsamic and honey, then sprinkle the sage leaves and the candied lemon over the top.

This is one of our most popular dishes at the restaurant; as the fresh goat's curd sits on the hot beetroots, fresh from our brick oven, it slowly melts to make an unctuous creamy sauce, so as you eat it the dish is slowly changing for the better. If you can get heritage beets, using all the different varieties, it's great, as the variety of colour really enhances the presentation.

Roasted Beetroot with Goat's Curd, Honeycomb and Watercress

Serves: 6

Preparation time: 20 minutes (providing the honeycomb is already made)

Cooking time: 2 hours

1kg uncooked beetroots

1 sprig of fresh thyme

1 sprig of fresh rosemary

4 garlic cloves

2 tablespoons olive oil

sea salt and freshly ground black pepper

1 tablespoon Confit Shallots (see page 217)

100ml Sherry Dressing (see page 216)

200g goat's curd

70g Honeycomb (see page 219)

100g watercress

Preheat your oven to 160°C/gas mark 3.

Wash the beetroots and pierce each one two or three times with a knife. Line a roasting tray with foil, put the beetroots in, add the thyme, rosemary and garlic and cover with more foil. Place in the oven and roast for about 1½ hours, or until a knife goes into the beetroots easily. Take off the foil and allow them to cool, then peel away the skin and discard along with the herbs and garlic (wearing disposable gloves to stop your fingers going pink). This can be done up to 2 days in advance.

Preheat your oven to 180°C/gas mark 4.

Arrange the beetroots in a roasting dish. If they are quite big, you can cut them into smaller pieces (2.5–5cm works best). Add the olive oil and make sure all the pieces are coated, then season with salt and pepper.

Place in the oven for 10 minutes, then remove and add the confit shallots and half the sherry dressing. Give a little mix, then spoon on the curd in tablespoon-size blobs and sprinkle pieces of honeycomb over. Garnish with the watercress, dressed with the rest of the sherry dressing.

I'm not sure what it is about charred broccoli and Caesar dressing, but it's a great combination that I come back to time and time again. It makes an interesting side for roast chicken, and it's also a good dish in itself.

Grilled Sprouting Broccoli with Caesar Dressing

Serves: 4

Preparation time: 15 minutes

Cooking time: 30 minutes

600g sprouting broccoli

sea salt

2 tablespoons olive oil

½ a lemon

4 tablespoons flaked almonds, toasted

For the Caesar dressing

4 tablespoons Mayonnaise (see page 217)

2 brown anchovy fillets, finely chopped

2 cloves of Confit Garlic (see page 217), peeled and ground to a paste

20g grated Parmesan cheese

To make the Caesar dressing, blend all the ingredients together and set aside.

Blanch the broccoli in salted boiling water for about a minute. Refresh in iced water and drain once cold.

Heat a griddle pan over a high heat (or you can use a barbecue). Put the broccoli into a mixing bowl and toss with the olive oil until well coated, then place on the griddle (depending on the size of your griddle you may need to cook the broccoli in batches). Don't worry if it gets dark marks – it really adds to the flavour.

When the broccoli is evenly coloured, place it in a mixing bowl. Add a squeeze of lemon and some sea salt. Pour over the Caesar dressing and toss. Transfer to serving plates and finish each one with a sprinkling of toasted almonds.

These work well on a barbecue, and they look fun too. Adjust the spices to suit your fancy.

Charred Corn on the Cob with Jerk Spices and Coconut

Makes: 6

Preparation time: 20 minutes

Cooking time: 40 minutes

6 corn on the cob

sea salt

1 teaspoon prepared jerk spice, toasted

1 chipotle en adobo from a jar

3 sprigs of fresh coriander, chopped

3 tablespoons Mayonnaise (see page 217)

100g desiccated coconut, toasted

Place the corn in a large saucepan, add a pinch of salt and cover with cold water. Bring to the boil, then lower the heat and simmer for 15 minutes.

Maintain a medium heat on your barbecue, or heat a griddle pan. Drain the corn, then place it direct on the barbecue or griddle on the stove over a medium heat. Don't be scared if it starts to get dark marks – it gives it a great flavour. When the corn is evenly coloured, take it off the heat and place it on a plate or chopping board.

Mix the toasted jerk spice, chipotle chilli and coriander into the mayo. Spread the mayo all over the corn cobs, until they are coated evenly, and finally roll each one in the toasted coconut. Eat straight away.

This is a great recipe to keep up your sleeve. It's amazing served simply with bread, in our pearl barley recipe (see page 23), or with fresh burrata or mozzarella. The tangy flavour goes with pretty much anything, and it lasts a while too. I always have a jar of this at home. Try adding freshly chopped basil just before using.

Peperonata

Makes: 1kg

Preparation time: 30 minutes

Cooking time: 1–1½ hours

100ml olive oil

6 red peppers, deseeded and sliced 5mm thick

2 red onions, finely sliced

2 garlic cloves, finely chopped

sea salt and freshly ground black pepper

10 plum tomatoes, deseeded and sliced

1 bay leaf

2 sprigs of fresh thyme

2 tablespoons demerara sugar

100ml red wine vinegar

finely grated zest of 1 lemon

Heat the oil in a large saucepan, then add the peppers, onions and garlic and cook gently for 15–20 minutes without colouring. Season with salt and pepper, then add the rest of the ingredients and continue to cook until the mixture has a nice semi-thick sauce consistency. Keep an eye on it and stir it often, to make sure it doesn't burn.

Remove the bay leaf and thyme, and store in a sterilized jar in the fridge until you need it. This will keep for up to 1 month.

Artichokes are one of my favourite vegetables, and this is one that works well on the barbecue too. Try using a different cheese, or swapping the bacon for chorizo or n'duja.

Roasted Artichokes with Caerphilly Crumble

Serves: 4
Preparation time: 1 hour
Cooking time: 45 minutes

2 globe artichokes

1 lemon

4 rashers of smoked streaky bacon, cut into 1cm pieces

1 tablespoon Confit Shallots (see page 217)

2 cloves of Confit Garlic (see page 217)

4 slices of white bread, crusts removed, cut into 1cm cubes

100g Caerphilly cheese, crumbled

1 sprig of fresh parsley, chopped

1 leaf of fresh chives, chopped

olive oil

freshly ground black pepper

You will also need a steamer

Set up a steamer ready for the artichokes.

Trim the end of each artichoke, about 2.5cm down (not the stalk end, the bulbous end). Cut the lemon in half and rub the area of artichoke you cut to prevent it going brown, then continue to do so every time you make a cut. Trim the outside leaves to make them square, not pointy. Peel the stem of each artichoke with a peeler or a knife, then cut about 5cm from the artichoke heart and discard. Cut the artichokes in half and then, with a spoon, scoop out the centre feathery bit and the smallest leaves.

Put the artichokes into the steamer, cut side up, and steam for 20 minutes.

To make the stuffing, cook the bacon in a frying pan until the fat comes out, then add the confit shallots and confit garlic. Add the bread cubes – the idea is that the bread absorbs the fat, which essentially contains the flavour. Allow the bread to take a little colour at this stage too. Transfer the contents of the pan to a mixing bowl and add the cheese and herbs.

Preheat your oven to 180°C/gas mark 4.

Put 2 tablespoons of the stuffing mix into the centre of each artichoke, where you removed the inner leaves. Drizzle with olive oil and a twist of black pepper, and place in the oven (or on the barbecue) for about 10–12 minutes, or until nice and browned.

New season's asparagus, crispy meat and a runny egg are a combination to die for. Here, we have taken out the more familiar pancetta or Serrano ham, and use chicken skin instead. And rather than use a poached egg, we slowly confit an egg yolk in olive oil, which really brings the dish together. Try adding wild mushrooms to the foaming butter with the asparagus when in season – morels would be perfect.

Asparagus with Crispy Chicken Skin and Confit Egg Yolk

Serves: 4

Preparation time: 20 minutes

Cooking time: 2 hours

120g chicken skin (approximately 4 breasts' or legs' worth)

sea salt and freshly ground black pepper

2 bunches of asparagus

4 egg yolks

olive oil, to cover

20g butter

1 handful of pea shoots

1 teaspoon Sherry Dressing (see page 216)

The chicken skin and the asparagus can be prepared in advance.

Preheat your oven to 180°C/gas mark 4.

Line a baking sheet with baking paper and spread the pieces of skin out so they are completely flat. Season with salt, then cover with another sheet of baking paper. If you have another baking sheet, place it on top so the pieces of skin stay flat and thin. If not, don't worry; they will just curl up a bit. Place in the oven for about 20 minutes (each oven is different, though, so check every 5 minutes to make sure the skin is not burning). You're looking for a crisp skin that's golden brown. Take out and cool on a rack.

Prepare your asparagus by removing the little ears on the stalks (some people like to peel it with a peeler, but I think this gives too much waste) and cutting about 5cm from the base (where it begins to be woody). Blanch the asparagus in salted boiling water for about 30 seconds, then refresh in iced water and drain.

To confit the egg yolks, preheat your oven to 65°C/gas as low as possible, an hour before serving. Separate the eggs, making sure all the white and membrane is removed, then place the yolks in an ovenproof dish and add enough olive oil to cover them completely. Place in the oven for 40 minutes, or longer if you prefer a firmer yolk.

Heat a large frying pan and add the butter. When it starts to foam, add the asparagus and allow to colour a little, but no more than 3 minutes.

To serve, arrange your asparagus on a plate, with a confit egg yolk in the centre and shards of crispy chicken skin around. Season with a little salt and pepper and finish with the pea shoots, and drizzle all over with the sherry dressing.

This is one of my favourite spring recipes, bursting with flavour and colour; it really gets you in the mood for summer. The flavour of the concentrated tomatoes does make a difference, but if you don't have time to make them, try using half fresh and half sun-dried.

Grilled Asparagus with Pink Grapefruit Sauce Vierge

Serves: 6

Preparation time: 1 day

Cooking time: 5 minutes

20 cherry tomatoes

sea salt and freshly ground black pepper

100ml olive oil

1 pink grapefruit

20 fresh basil leaves

2 tablespoons Confit Shallots (see page 217)

1 clove of Confit Garlic (see page 217)

20ml sherry vinegar

3 bunches of asparagus

3 tablespoons Balsamic Glaze (see page 217)

Preheat your oven to its lowest setting.

Cut each tomato in half and put them on a baking sheet lined with baking paper, cut side up. Season with salt, pepper and a drizzle of olive oil and put into the oven on the lowest setting for a couple of hours, or until dried. You can turn the oven off and leave the tomatoes in the oven to dry out overnight; the slower you dry them, the better.

When the tomatoes are dried, roughly chop them into 5mm pieces and place in a small mixing bowl. Segment the grapefruit and chop into similar-size pieces. Add the grapefruit to the tomatoes, then add the 100ml olive oil, 12 of the basil leaves, the confit shallots, garlic and sherry vinegar and stir with a spoon. Set aside while you start the asparagus.

Prepare your asparagus by removing the little ears from the stalks (some people like to peel with a peeler, but I think this gives too much waste) and cutting about 5cm from the base (where it begins to be woody). Blanch in salted boiling water for about 30 seconds, then refresh in iced water and drain.

Heat a griddle pan over a high heat. Lightly oil and season your asparagus. Grill for a couple of minutes, or until you have nice char lines, rotating the spears so they are coloured and cooked all over.

Arrange the asparagus on plates with the sauce spooned around, and finish with the rest of the basil leaves. A little of that magical balsamic glaze drizzled over at this stage really lifts the dish.

Piedmont's answer to fondue, bagna cauda is a northern Italian classic. Normally used for dipping vegetables, I like to pair it with roasted cauliflower and finish with tangy pickled walnuts to cut the richness. Traditionally it's quite pungent in the garlic department, but you can add or subtract, as you like (I use confit garlic to soften it a little).

Roasted Cauliflower with Bagna Cauda and Pickled Walnuts

Serves: 4

Preparation time: 10 minutes

Cooking time: 25 minutes

sea salt

1 large cauliflower, cut into florets

150ml olive oil, the best you can get

1 sprig of fresh rosemary

4 cloves of Confit Garlic (see page 217)

10 brown anchovy fillets

110g unsalted butter, cut into 2cm cubes

8 pickled walnuts (best to buy them ready-pickled in a jar)

To garnish

2 handfuls of watercress

1 tablespoon Sherry Dressing (see page 216)

Bring a saucepan of salted water to the boil, then add your cauliflower and blanch for 1 minute. Refresh in iced water, then drain and dry.

Preheat your oven to 160°C/gas mark 3. Place the cauliflower florets in a roasting tray and lightly drizzle with 30ml of the olive oil. Add the rosemary and place in the oven for about 25 minutes, or until lightly browned.

In the meantime, make the bagna cauda. Put the garlic, anchovies and the remaining 120ml of olive oil into a saucepan and whisk together over a medium heat. Add the butter, 5–6 cubes at a time, and whisk continuously so the mixture emulsifies and becomes creamy.

When the cauliflower is ready, remove from the oven and divide between your serving plates. Drizzle the bagna cauda over and around, and place 2 pickled walnuts, broken with your fingers, on top. Garnish with the watercress, dressed with the sherry dressing.

The vegetables are the stars of the show here, with the lardo more of a middle man to bring all the flavours together. If you have a farm shop nearby, go and see them, as they will have the best produce for this. If you can't get lardo, try using Parma ham instead – it has way less fat content, so you may need to add a touch of olive oil, but it will give a nice pork flavour.

Slow-roasted Heritage Carrots with Lardo, Peas and Mint

Serves: 4

Preparation time: 20 minutes

Cooking time: 20 minutes

8 heritage carrots, about 15cm long

sea salt and freshly ground black pepper

4 slices of lardo, about 12 x 6cm, 2mm thick

1 tablespoon Confit Shallots (see page 217)

2 cloves of Confit Garlic (see page 217)

150g fresh shelled English peas (or frozen if not in season), blanched and refreshed

200ml Chicken Stock (see page 216)

20ml olive oil

40g butter

8 fresh mint leaves

Cut the green stems off the carrots, but feel free to leave a little of them on if you like, for presentation. Peel and halve the carrots lengthways, then blanch in salted boiling water for about 5 minutes, depending on size (a knife should go through with a little pressure), then refresh in iced water.

Put a sauté pan over a medium heat. Add the lardo and allow to melt so that it releases its fat. Add the confit shallots and garlic, season with salt and pepper, then add the peas and give a good stir. Now add the chicken stock and turn up the heat so it reduces rapidly.

To serve, put another sauté pan over a medium heat and add the olive oil. Add the carrots and let them lightly brown, turning them as they colour. When almost done, add 20g of the butter and allow it to foam and give the carrots a nutty flavour.

When the chicken stock has reduced by three-quarters, add the remaining 20g of butter, lower the heat and give it a good stir to emulsify and enrich the ragout. Remove any lardo that hasn't melted and discard. Finely chop the mint and stir into the ragout. Arrange the carrots on a warm serving plate and spoon the ragout over and around.

This raw dish has been on the menu at the restaurant since day one, and people seem to love it. Anything raw or 'crudo' needs to have three basic elements – salt, oil and acidity. Then you can add textures, spices or herbs as you wish. This is great for a chef, because as long as you have each element in the dish, you can be as creative as you like. For example, instead of seasoning with salt, we use a salt brick as a plate, so the fish absorbs the seasoning. Salt can also come in the form of capers or samphire, and acidity with lime or sherry vinegar and so on.

Tuna with Watermelon, Balsamic and Basil

Serves: 4

Preparation time: 10 minutes (or prepare the watermelon the day before)

Cooking time: 5 minutes

50g caster sugar

50ml water

1 red chilli (seeds removed if you don't want too much of a kick), roughly chopped

100g watermelon, skinned and cut into 1cm cubes

1 piece of fresh tuna, approximately 200g, or the size of a chocolate bar. (If you can't get it in the shape of a bar, you can buy a tuna steak and cut it into cubes instead – see method)

Balsamic Glaze (see page 217)

fresh basil leaves

sea salt

The watermelon gets better with time, so while you can make and eat this right away, if you are able to prepare the watermelon the day before, the flavour becomes much deeper. Put the sugar and water into a saucepan and bring to the boil. Remove from the heat and add the chilli. Allow to cool. When cold, add the watermelon cubes. These can now be used right away or be left in the fridge to marinate until the next day.

Slice the tuna 3mm thick and spread out on a plate. Put a cube of watermelon on top of each slice. Add a drizzle of balsamic glaze and some leaves of basil, cut into 1cm pieces, to each one. Finish with sea salt and eat immediately.

If using a tuna steak, cut the tuna into 1cm dice and place in a mixing bowl. Add 1 teaspoon of watermelon cubes per 1 tablespoon of tuna. Add the basil, season and mix. Divide between serving plates and finish with a drizzle of balsamic glaze.

Serves: 4

Preparation time: 20 minutes

Cooking time: 1 hour

For the lobster cream sauce

1 lobster carcass

50ml olive oil

2 shallots, chopped

2 garlic cloves, crushed

1 stick of celery,
cut into 1cm pieces

1 sprig of fresh thyme

1 bay leaf

1 tablespoon tomato purée

1 glass of white wine

200ml Chicken Stock
(see page 216), or vegetable stock

500ml double cream, or enough
to cover

sea salt and freshly ground
black pepper

For the fishballs

500g pollock, or any other white
fish, such as haddock, cod or hake,
skinned and cut into 2.5cm pieces

2 egg whites

1 sprig of fresh tarragon

1 sprig of fresh parsley

1 leaf of fresh chives

grated zest of 1 lemon

To finish

100g butter

100g fresh breadcrumbs

100g Parmesan cheese, grated

This dish came about when we had grilled lobster on the menu, and were using perfect squares of pollock for another dish. To prevent any waste, we made a cream sauce from the lobster shells, and used the pollock trimmings to make fishballs. It's so popular now that we are buying the fish and lobster specifically for this; it's real comfort food and goes well with our homemade breads. The sauce is great with pasta too, or as a base for a fish pie.

Cornish Pollock Fishballs with Lobster Cream and Parmesan

First, make the sauce. Take the lobster carcass and, using scissors, break it into 5 or 6 pieces. Put the olive oil into a large saucepan over a medium heat, and when hot, add the pieces of lobster shell. Cook for about 8 minutes, or until they dry out and start to colour a little.

Add the shallots, garlic, celery, thyme and bay leaf and continue to cook for a further 5 minutes. Add the tomato purée, mix well, and continue to cook over a medium heat, without colour, for 5 minutes. Add the wine and simmer until reduced by three-quarters, then add the stock and reduce by three-quarters again. Add the cream, lower the heat to a simmer and cook for 30 minutes. Strain through a sieve, and correct the seasoning.

Next, make the fishballs. Put the fish and egg whites into a blender and blend until smooth. Transfer the mixture to a bowl and add the herbs and lemon zest. Season with salt and pepper. Roll into golfball-size balls and refrigerate until you are ready to cook.

Melt the butter in a frying pan over a medium heat and add the breadcrumbs. Toast until golden brown, stirring often. If they start to colour too quickly, lower the heat. Allow to cool.

Preheat your oven to 180°C/gas mark 4. Put the fishballs into an earthenware baking dish, evenly spaced out, and pour over the sauce. Place in the oven for about 12 minutes, then take out, sprinkle over the Parmesan, and return to the oven for a further 5 minutes.

Just before serving, sprinkle with 3–4 tablespoons of the browned breadcrumbs.

Playing with the three basic components of 'crudo' or raw dishes (salt, oil and acidity), we use pickled shimeji mushrooms and lime for acidity, blueberry and truffle to give a sweet earthiness and finish with rocket leaves or rocket cress for a nice peppery punch. The colours are striking, and it tastes pretty good too.

Halibut Tartare with Blueberries and Pickled Mushrooms

Serves: 4

Preparation time: 3 hours, 20 minutes

Cooking time: 10 minutes

16 shimeji mushrooms, or 4 shiitake if you can't find shimeji

Pickling Liquid, enough to cover (see page 216)

200g blueberries

juice of ½ a lemon

500g very fresh halibut fillet, skinned

a squeeze of lime juice

sea salt

rocket cress, to garnish (rocket leaves are fine too)

1 teaspoon truffle oil

4 slices of sourdough bread, toasted

First, pickle the mushrooms. This can be done well in advance, as the longer you can leave them to pickle, the better. You need 16 mushrooms for this recipe, but you can pickle them in larger numbers – they will keep for up to 1 month. Bring the pickling liquid to the boil. Have your mushrooms ready in a sterilized jar or jars, then pour the hot pickling liquid over them and seal. Leave for at least 3 hours before using.

To make the blueberry coulis, put the blueberries into a small saucepan with the lemon juice, bring to the boil, then lower the heat and simmer until reduced to a thick compote. Scrape through a fine sieve, then allow to cool. It will taste very sharp, but that's fine – it's all part of the plan.

When ready to serve, slice the halibut into 5mm cubes and place them in a chilled mixing bowl. Add 3 teaspoons of the blueberry coulis, a squeeze of lime and a pinch of sea salt. Give a good mix, and place on a serving plate. Garnish with the pickled shimeji, some rocket cress or rocket leaves, and drizzle the truffle oil around. Serve with warm toast on the side.

I love how well octopus and chorizo go together, and with salty capers and sharp lemon segments, this dish has it all. After it had been on the menu for about a year, we decided to add some new potatoes – they caramelize in the oils from the chorizo and really help the balance of the dish. If octopus is too hard to find, try using squid. You won't need to precook it, just add it raw with the chorizo in the final step.

Roasted Octopus with Chorizo, Potato and Caper Berries

Serves: 4

Preparation time: 1 hour

Cooking time: about 1 hour

1 daikon radish

1 octopus, approximately 1kg, cleaned (ask your fishmonger to remove the head)

1 onion

2 sticks of celery

2 carrots

1 bay leaf

1 sprig of fresh thyme

10 black peppercorns

200ml red wine

2 tablespoons olive oil

10 new potatoes, cooked and halved

250g cooking chorizo sausage, skinned and cut into 1cm dice

2 tablespoons Confit Shallots (see page 217)

1 lemon, segmented

1 sprig of fresh parsley, finely chopped

sea salt and freshly ground black pepper

2 pinches of caper berries, deep-fried for 30 seconds until crisp, to garnish

To prepare the octopus, we do something a little different from usual to tenderize it. First, cut the daikon radish in half and rub the cut ends all over the octopus. The enzymes in the daikon help to tenderize the octopus, which can be incredibly tough. Then we massage – sounds crazy, I know. Basically, give a little pull at 2.5cm intervals all the way down each tentacle.

Place your massaged and rubbed octopus in a large saucepan, and add the onion, celery, carrots, herbs and peppercorns. Pour in the wine and enough cold water to cover and slowly bring to the boil. Lower the heat and simmer for about 45–60 minutes, or until the octopus is tender. Allow it to cool in the stock, then remove to a board, taking care as the skin is delicate and can come away. Cut into 2.5cm pieces, discarding the vegetables.

When ready to serve, heat the olive oil in a frying pan. Add the potatoes and the pieces of octopus and lightly brown. Next add the chorizo and cook until the fats are released. Sauté together for 2–3 minutes, then add the confit shallots, lemon segments and parsley. Give everything a good mix and allow get to know each other for a few minutes, then plate up, seasoning with salt and pepper and garnishing with the crispy capers.

I love oysters whether straight up or cooked. There are some great classic ways of cooking oysters in every cuisine. This dish was inspired by a conversation with one of our regulars. While catching up and discussing the menu, I mentioned how good I thought our Irish oysters were. On hearing that they only ate cooked oysters, and knowing the flavours they liked, I had a play around and this ended up on the menu.

Grilled Oysters with Spicy Bacon Butter

Serves: 2–3

Preparation time: 10 minutes

Cooking time: 10 minutes

6 of the best, freshest oysters you can find

3 rashers of smoked streaky bacon, or pancetta if you can find it, cut into 2.5mm lardons

50g butter

1 tablespoon Confit Shallots (see page 217)

a few splashes of Tabasco

½ a lemon

1 sprig of fresh parsley, finely chopped

2 tablespoons breadcrumbs

First, open your oysters carefully and place them on a tray. If you're unsure how to open them, it's best to look at a video on the internet – describing how to do it here could be tricky and I'd hate you to waste an oyster! Preheat your grill to a medium-hot temperature.

To make the butter, place a frying pan over a medium heat. Add the bacon and cook for a few minutes until it's a little crisp and brown. Next, add the butter and wait for it to begin to foam. Add the shallots and give a good stir. Let the butter continue to cook until almost nutty brown, then add a few splashes of Tabasco to your taste. Soon after this the butter will become a nutty brown, so take off the heat and squeeze the lemon over. It will splutter a little, so be careful.

Finish the sauce with the chopped parsley, then spoon 1 tablespoon over each oyster. Sprinkle each one with breadcrumbs and place under the grill for 1–2 minutes.

Be careful when eating, as the oyster shell can be quite warm.

This is what we call a one-pot wonder – it's so easy to make, and is tasty as hell. In my opinion this dish represents what cooking and eating is all about: great produce, cooked simply and eaten with your sleeves rolled up and a couple of slices of bread to mop up the juices. If you live in London, make the trip to Billingsgate Market – it's well worth the 4 a.m. start, and the fry-up in the café at the end is pretty damn good. You'll see the freshest seafood around, and plenty of interesting characters to boot.

Roasted Crab Claws with Garlic Butter

Serves: 2
Preparation time: 10 minutes
Cooking time: 10 minutes

4 crab claws, approximately 10cm long
sea salt and freshly ground black pepper
50g butter
3 garlic cloves, crushed
½ a lemon
1 sprig of fresh parsley, chopped

To serve
1 handful of watercress
1 teaspoon Sherry Dressing (see page 216)
fresh bread

If you've managed to get fresh crab claws, they will need to be boiled in salted water for 5 minutes, then refreshed in ice. If you couldn't make the voyage to Billingsgate and are using cooked or frozen claws, then skip this stage – just make sure you defrost them overnight.

Preheat your oven to 200°C/gas mark 6. When ready to go, put an ovenproof frying pan on the stove and heat it to a medium temperature.

Tap each claw firmly with the back of a knife, to create a crack. Do this between every joint. This is important, as it allows the butter to really get inside. Now put the claws, butter and garlic into the hot pan and let things get started. Once the butter starts to foam, place the pan in the oven for 5–10 minutes, or until the claws are hot through.

Remove from the oven, squeeze the lemon juice over and season with salt and pepper, then lift the claws out and transfer to a serving plate. Give the garlicky butter a good stir, add the parsley, then pour all over the crab. Garnish with the watercress, dressed with the sherry dressing, and serve with fresh bread.

Like the Smoked Haddock Scotch Eggs (opposite), this dish takes its inspiration from kedgeree. The chowder is more of a rainy-day variation, ideal for warming your cockles. We slow-cook our eggs at 63°C for 45 minutes, but if you don't have the equipment to regulate the temperature to precisely 63°C, you can cook a traditional poached egg.

Smoked Haddock Chowder with a Poached Egg and Puffed Rice

Serves: 4

Preparation time: 20 minutes

Cooking time: 45 minutes

vegetable oil, for deep-frying

4 eggs

50ml olive oil

2 onions, finely chopped

2 carrots, finely chopped

2 sticks of celery, finely chopped

1 leek, finely chopped

4 potatoes, cut into 1cm dice

1 bay leaf

sea salt and freshly ground black pepper

2 glasses of white wine

500ml Chicken Stock (see page 216)

500ml double cream

600g smoked haddock, skinned, pin-boned and cut into 1cm cubes

1 handful of dry, parboiled long-grain rice (I use Uncle Ben's)

a pinch of curry powder

1 sprig of fresh parsley, chopped

1 leaf of fresh chives, chopped

1 sprig of fresh coriander, chopped

Heat the vegetable oil to 180°C in your deep-fat fryer or in a heavy-based saucepan.

If slow-cooking the eggs, set your water bath to 63°C and when the temperature is reached, add the eggs (in the shell) and leave for 45 minutes. You can use them straight away, or chill in iced water and refrigerate for later.

Heat the olive oil in a frying pan and cook the onions, carrots, celery, leek, potatoes and bay leaf until soft, with no colour. Season with salt and pepper. Add the white wine and simmer until reduced by three-quarters, then add the chicken stock and continue to simmer until reduced by half.

Add the cream, bring to a simmer, then add the haddock and cook for approximately 15 minutes, or until the soup begins to thicken and the potatoes are cooked. Remove from the stove and set aside to cool if you're not eating right away.

To make the puffed rice, gently drop the parboiled rice into your deep-fat fryer or saucepan and after 30 seconds–1 minute you will see it puff up like rice crispies. Remove the rice with a tea strainer and drain on kitchen paper. Sprinkle with salt and a pinch of curry powder.

Bring a saucepan of water to the boil for your eggs. Crack your slow-cooked eggs into the water and reheat, or poach your eggs in the traditional way.

To serve the chowder, remove the bay leaf, bring to the boil, add the chopped herbs, and divide between serving dishes. Place an egg in each one, then sprinkle with a good pinch of puffed rice. When eating, break the egg and give it a mix – it makes all the difference.

This is a dish that comes and goes at the restaurant, and our regulars love it when it makes a return. A play on kedgeree, one of the wonderful dishes the British brought back from India, it goes great with a hoppy IPA, also of the same heritage, as extra hops were added to beer to make it last the voyage from England to Bombay.

Smoked Haddock Scotch Egg with Curried Mayonnaise

Makes: 8

Preparation time: 2½ hours

Cooking time: 10 minutes

8 eggs

600g smoked haddock, skinned and pin-boned

2 egg whites

pinch of sea salt

4 spring onions, finely sliced

2 sprigs of fresh coriander, chopped

2 small red chillies, deseeded and chopped

½ teaspoon pickled ginger from a jar

a pinch of cayenne pepper

100g plain flour

2 eggs, beaten

200g panko breadcrumbs

vegetable oil, for deep-frying

For the curried mayonnaise

2 tablespoons Mayonnaise (see page 217)

a pinch of curry powder, lightly toasted

1 sprig of fresh coriander, chopped

1 sprig of fresh mint, chopped

You will also need a deep-fat fryer

Cook the eggs in boiling water for 7 minutes, then refresh in iced water. Peel the eggs, then set aside.

Put the smoked haddock into a food processor with the egg whites and salt, and blend together. Transfer to a mixing bowl and add the spring onions, coriander, chillies, ginger and cayenne pepper. You can reduce or omit the chillies and cayenne if you are not too enthusiastic on the spice front. Give it all a good mix.

Take a plum-size ball of the mixture, with wet hands to stop it sticking, and flatten it out to approximately 1cm thick. Wrap the haddock mix around one of the peeled eggs, using a bit more of the mixture if you need to fill any gaps. Repeat with the rest of the eggs. Place them on a plate lined with kitchen paper to absorb any moisture, and put into the fridge for 2 hours to firm up.

Get your flour, eggs and breadcrumbs ready in three separate bowls and remove the eggs from the fridge. Roll each one in the flour, then coat in the beaten eggs and lastly roll in the breadcrumbs.

Mix all the ingredients for the curried mayonnaise together in a bowl.

Heat the oil to 170°C in your deep-fat fryer and cook your Scotch eggs for 7 minutes, or until golden brown. Drain on kitchen paper, then when cool enough to handle, cut each one in half. Serve with a good dollop of curried mayonnaise.

Serves: 4

Preparation time: 30 minutes

Cooking time: 3 hours

For the cuttlefish

1kg cuttlefish, cleaned

100ml olive oil

2 onions, chopped

2 sticks of celery, chopped

1 carrot, chopped

1 head of fennel, chopped

2 bay leaves

1 sprig of fresh thyme

3 garlic cloves, crushed

300ml red wine

1 (400g) tin of chopped tomatoes

Chicken Stock (see page 216), or enough to cover

For the charred fennel

2 heads of fennel

50ml olive oil

2 garlic cloves, crushed

1 chilli, deseeded and roughly chopped

1 sprig of fresh rosemary

sea salt and freshly ground black pepper

For the risotto

100ml olive oil

1 onion, finely chopped

2 sticks of celery, finely chopped

1 garlic clove, finely chopped

1 red chilli, deseeded and finely chopped

1 sprig of fresh thyme

1 bay leaf

350g Arborio risotto rice

600ml Chicken Stock (see page 216)

2 sprigs of fresh parsley, finely chopped

2 tablespoons chilli oil

I love this dish – I learnt how to cook cuttlefish when I did a two-week stage at the Anchor & Hope on The Cut near Waterloo, one of the best gastro-pubs in the country. I don't remember their recipe exactly; I just remember the love and care that went into it. After making it at home for a few years, this is the recipe that works best (just don't forget the love). When in season, wild garlic instead of parsley at the end works a treat.

Cuttlefish Risotto with Charred Fennel

Ask your fishmonger to prepare the cuttlefish for you, keeping the ink sac separate. Cut the cuttlefish into 5cm pieces.

To cook the cuttlefish, heat 50ml olive oil in a frying pan, add the onions, celery, carrot, fennel, bay leaves, thyme and garlic, and cook gently until softened. Meanwhile, in another frying pan, seal the cuttlefish in 50ml olive oil until lightly golden. When the vegetables are tender, add the red wine and simmer until reduced by half. Add the cuttlefish and the tinned tomatoes and pour in enough chicken stock to cover. Bring to the boil, then lower the heat to a simmer.

At this point, carefully open the reserved ink sac (wearing gloves) and add to the stew. The ink will give it a beautiful deep colour. Cover with a lid and cook for 1 hour, or until the cuttlefish is tender, then leave to cool in the stock. When cool, strain the cuttlefish, discarding the vegetables, and reserve the liquid for later.

To make the charred fennel, preheat your oven to 180°C/gas mark 4 and heat a griddle on the stove. Cut each piece of fennel into 8 segments and put them into a bowl with the olive oil, garlic, chilli and rosemary. Season and mix well. Griddle the fennel until dark, then transfer to a roasting tray with the garlic, oil and chilli from the bowl. Roast for 10 minutes, then remove from the oven and reserve for later.

To make the risotto, heat the olive oil and sweat the onion, celery, garlic, chilli, thyme and bay leaf, taking care they don't colour. Season with salt and pepper. Add the risotto rice and stir to coat gently in the olive oil. Now start adding the stock gradually, beginning with the cuttlefish stock and then, when that's finished, using the chicken stock, allowing the rice to absorb it all before you add more. You may not need to use all the chicken stock, depending on how much the cuttlefish stock has reduced when cooking.

As soon as the rice is tender, add the cuttlefish and bring up to temperature. Remove the bay leaf and thyme. Finish with the chopped parsley, then divide between serving plates and garnish each one with a piece of charred fennel and a drizzle of chilli oil.

I was inspired to create this dish after tasting the smoked vodka from James Chase. He dropped off a sample bottle at the restaurant and it was such an interesting flavour that we started playing around with it, and naturally Russian flavours came to mind. Non-smoked vodka works here too, and you can try swapping the pickled cucumber for pickled beets as well.

Mackerel Tartare with Smoked Vodka and Pickled Cucumber

Serves: 4

Preparation time: 20 minutes (if the cucumber is already pickled, otherwise 2 hours–3 days)

Cooking time: none

¼ of a cucumber, peeled and deseeded, cut into 2mm dice

100ml Pickling Liquid (see page 216)

4 fresh mackerel fillets, skinned and pin-boned

1 shallot, finely chopped

1 leaf of fresh chives, finely chopped

1 tablespoon smoked vodka

sea salt

4 teaspoons crème fraîche

8 fresh coriander leaves

sourdough bread, toasted

First, pickle your cucumber. This is best done 3 days in advance, but if you are short of time, a couple of hours will be fine too. Simply cover the cucumber with the pickling liquid and allow it to work its magic.

When ready to serve, slice the mackerel into 5mm cubes and place it in a mixing bowl. Drain the pickled cucumber and add to the bowl, then add the shallot, chives and smoked vodka and season with salt.

Divide between serving plates, and finish each one with a teaspoon of crème fraîche and a couple of coriander leaves. Serve with fresh sourdough toast.

This is a dish from our opening restaurant menu and made me fall in love with n'duja – a spreadable spicy sausage. It comes from Calabria in the south of Italy, and is almost as fiery as the people of the region – you can sneak it into pretty much any dish, and this one is no exception.

Mussels and Clams with N'duja and Fennel Broth

Serves: 4
Preparation time: 20 minutes
Cooking time: 40 minutes

300g mussels
300g clams
150g n'duja, skin removed
olive oil
2 garlic cloves, crushed
3 shallots, finely chopped
1 glass of white wine
4 sprigs of fresh parsley, chopped

For the fennel broth
8 heads of baby fennel, or 2 heads of regular fennel, thinly sliced 2mm thick
olive oil
500ml Chicken Stock (see page 216)
1 tablespoon Confit Shallots (see page 217)
1 sprig of fresh thyme
1 bay leaf
10 fennel seeds, crushed
a pinch of saffron

Ask your fishmonger to clean your mussels and clams, removing the beards and any barnacles. Roll the n'duja into 1cm balls.

Remove the herb tops from the fennel, finely chop and reserve for later.

To make the fennel broth, heat a drizzle of olive oil in a frying pan, add the fennel and cook until brown. Transfer to a saucepan, cover with the chicken stock, then add the other broth ingredients and simmer for 30 minutes.

When ready to serve, put a large saucepan over a medium heat. Add a splash of olive oil, the mussels and clams, n'duja, garlic and shallots and turn the heat up to high. As the n'duja starts to colour, add the wine and allow to reduce. Add the broth, including the fennel, and cook for a few minutes until all the mussels and clams are open. Discard any that remain closed. Finish with chopped parsley and the chopped fennel tops.

Serves: 6
Preparation time: 1 day
Cooking time: 1 ½ hours

For the salt cod

50g sea salt

finely grated zest of ½ a lemon

1 garlic clove, sliced

300g fresh cod fillet

1 sprig of fresh thyme

For the brandade

300g salt cod (see above)

500ml milk

300g potatoes, peeled and cut into 2cm cubes

1 bay leaf

4 cloves of Confit Garlic (see page 217)

200ml olive oil

10g capers, finely chopped

1 sprig of fresh parsley, chopped

1 leaf of fresh chives, chopped

½ a lemon

For the charred tomato jam

6 plum tomatoes, halved

50ml olive oil

2 shallots, finely chopped

1 sprig of fresh thyme

1 sprig of fresh rosemary

2 garlic cloves, finely chopped

1 chilli, halved, deseeded and finely chopped

1 tablespoon tomato purée

50g caster sugar

50ml red wine vinegar

toasted bread, to serve

Based on the traditional French brandade de morue, this has been adapted a little: we use fresh cod that has been home-salted rather than the traditional salt cod, which is super-dry and needs rehydrating for a few days, with regular water changes. This recipe is less aggressive than the French version, and we add capers and fresh herbs to jazz up the flavour a little. Buy the best olive oil you can – it makes all the difference.

Whipped Brandade with Charred Tomato Jam

First, salt the fish, which needs to be started a day in advance. Sprinkle half the salt over the bottom of a bowl and add half the lemon zest and garlic. Sit the fish on top, cover with the rest of the salt, lemon zest and garlic, and add the thyme. Cover the bowl with clingfilm and put into the fridge for 24 hours.

When you are ready to cook, preheat your oven to 200°C/gas mark 6. Put the tomatoes into a roasting tray and drizzle with 25ml of the olive oil. Place in the oven for about 20 minutes, or until the tomatoes start to blacken.

Heat the remaining 25ml of olive oil in a saucepan, add the shallots, thyme, rosemary, garlic and chilli, and cook gently until soft, with no colour. Add the tomatoes and tomato purée and cook for a further 10 minutes. Add the sugar and vinegar, then lower the heat and allow to slowly bubble away until the mixture is thick, like a jam (approximately 45 minutes). Remove from the heat, pass through a fine sieve and allow to cool.

To make the brandade, take the cod from the fridge and wash off the salt under cold water. Dry with kitchen paper and place in a clean saucepan. Cover with the milk, then add the potatoes and the bay leaf and gently simmer until the potatoes are cooked.

Strain the fish and potatoes and place in a mixing bowl. Add the garlic, then break it all down with a spoon until a rough mash is formed. Slowly start adding the oil, beating it in. When all the oil has been absorbed, add the capers and herbs and a squeeze of lemon juice. Serve with freshly toasted bread, with the jam on the side.

This dish is all about accentuating the pure flavours of the ingredients, by cooking them in a scallop shell sealed with bread dough, so none of them can escape. Try using pumpkin purée instead of mash, or, if you have bigger shells, add some clams too. There are plenty of ways to vary this dish.

Scallops Baked in the Shell

Serves: 4

Preparation time: 30 minutes

Cooking time: 1½ hours

1 onion, roughly chopped

1 carrot, roughly chopped

2 sticks of celery

10g dried Irish sea dulse

5g saffron strands

1 bay leaf

500ml Chicken Stock
(see page 216)

10 mussels, cleaned

2 potatoes, peeled and
cut into 2cm cubes

sea salt and freshly ground
black pepper

20g butter

4 hand-dived scallops,
in their shells

100g plain flour mixed with
just enough water to bind

To garnish

fresh basil leaves

extra virgin olive oil

First, make the stock. Put the onion, carrot, celery, sea dulse, saffron and bay leaf into a large saucepan, and add the chicken stock. Bring to the boil, then lower the heat and simmer for 1 hour.

Strain the stock into a clean saucepan and bring back to the boil, then add the cleaned mussels and cook until they are all open (discard any that remain closed). Take out the mussels, pick the meat out of the shells, and set aside. Leave the stock to cool.

Next, make the mashed potato. Put the potatoes into a saucepan and cover with cold water. Add a good pinch of salt and gently bring to a simmer. When the potatoes are cooked, strain and purée. Add the butter and adjust the seasoning.

Use a shucking knife to prise the scallop shells apart and release the meat from the shells. Wash the scallops, then separate and discard the outer skirt, but keep the orange coral. Pat the white meat and coral dry on kitchen paper. Give your scallop shells a good scrub. Allow them to dry and put them on a baking tray.

Put a spoonful of the potato purée in the bottom of each shell, then place a raw scallop and coral on top, and a cooked mussel either side of the scallop. Pour 2 tablespoons of the stock over the scallop, and then place the other half of the scallop shell on top.

Take a piece of dough, the size of a plum, and roll it out in your hands until it's long enough to go around the circumference of the shell. Slowly work your way around the shell, making sure the lid is stuck to the base with the dough.

When ready to cook, preheat your oven to 180°C/gas mark 4 and cook the scallops for approximately 7–10 minutes. Cut through the baked dough to open the shell (be careful, they will be hot!). Ovens vary, so if the scallops come out a little undercooked, put them back in for a few extra minutes. Garnish with the basil leaves and a drizzle of olive oil.

I love how the Spanish and Italians cook shellfish with cured meat, whether it be pancetta or pata negra – the two go so well together. You find this in British cuisine too, with streaky bacon a wonderful substitute. Here we use two types of cured meat: guanciale, which is cured pig's cheek, and lardo, cured pig's fat from the back of the animal. The lardo melts into the breadcrumbs to give a lovely piggy flavour, and, with the crunchiness, a nice texture too. An Italian friend of mine once told me a wonderful thing about guanciale: 'When God shaves, guanciale comes off and falls down to earth.' Says it all really.

Steamed Clams with Guanciale, and a Lardo and Parsley Crumb

Serves: 4

Preparation time: 20 minutes

Cooking time: 20 minutes

80g thinly sliced lardo, or Parma ham if you can't get hold of lardo

100g breadcrumbs

2 pinches of chopped fresh parsley

8 slices of guanciale, or pancetta or Parma ham if you can't get hold of guanciale

1 tablespoon Confit Shallots (see page 217)

1 clove of Confit Garlic (see page 217)

1 sprig of fresh thyme

600g clams, cleaned

1 glass of white wine

100ml Chicken Stock (see page 216)

First make the lardo and parsley crumb. Heat a frying pan over a medium heat and add the lardo. Allow to cook so the fat is released, and when there are plenty of oils in the pan, add the breadcrumbs and lower the heat. Cook slowly for about 10 minutes, or until all the fat is absorbed and the crumbs are evenly golden brown. Allow to cool, then add the parsley. Remove any unmelted pieces of lardo and discard.

When ready to serve, heat a saucepan over a high heat. Add the guanciale and cook until golden brown. Next, add the shallots, garlic and thyme. Give it a good stir, still over a high heat, then add the clams and the white wine.

Allow the wine to reduce, then add the chicken stock and keep cooking until all the shells are open. (Discard any that remain closed.)

Serve in a big bowl, and sprinkle over the lardo crumb liberally.

This dish goes way back, to when Tom Cenci (our Senior Sous Chef) and I worked at Noble Rot, the sister restaurant to 1 Lombard Street, where we both trained. Julian, the chef, was one of the most influential people I have worked for – he's a loss to Britain, but a great gain for Canada, where he now cooks. We serve this a little differently at the restaurant to how we did back then, but it's always a winner.

Beef Carpaccio with Foie Gras

Serves: 6

Preparation time: 1 day

Cooking time: 30 minutes

300ml port

50g caster sugar

1 clove

1 star anise

300g foie gras

sea salt and freshly ground black pepper

a splash of Cognac

600g piece of centre cut beef fillet, trimmed

50g pecorino cheese

To make the port reduction, put the port, sugar and spices into a small saucepan and heat until the mixture has the consistency of runny honey. Strain and set aside to cool.

Next, we need to make the cured foie gras. Allow the foie gras to come to room temperature. Using a small spoon, start to explore inside and whenever you come across a vein, remove it. Shape it back together, place it on a plate and season with salt, pepper and a splash of Cognac. Put into the fridge and allow to firm up for a couple of hours.

Preheat your oven to 120°C/gas mark ½.

Put the foie gras into an ovenproof dish and place in the oven for approximately 10 minutes, or until it just starts to melt. Remove it from the oven and lift it out of the melted fat, then place it on a piece of clingfilm and roll it into a sausage about 2.5cm thick, and as long as your beef fillet. Tie each end and place in the freezer for a few hours until frozen. If you have more than one roll that's fine, you can freeze them for another time, or refrigerate and eat on toast.

Take your beef fillet and, using a wooden spoon or something similar, insert it down the centre to make a hole all the way in so it comes out the other side. Give it a little wiggle to make the hole wider, as this is where we will insert the roll of foie gras. Remove the clingfilm from the foie gras, then insert the roll into the hole in the beef. Wrap the whole thing in clingfilm again.

If you don't have a slicing machine, refrigerate the beef until firm, then carefully slice as thinly as possible. If you do have access to a slicing machine, freeze the beef overnight. When ready to serve, remove the beef from the freezer and allow to stand for 20 minutes (this will make it easier to slice). Slice the beef 2.5mm thick.

Arrange the beef on a serving platter, about 8 slices per person, with the slices of foie gras on top. Drizzle over the port reduction and grate over the pecorino, as finely as possible. Season with salt and pepper and enjoy.

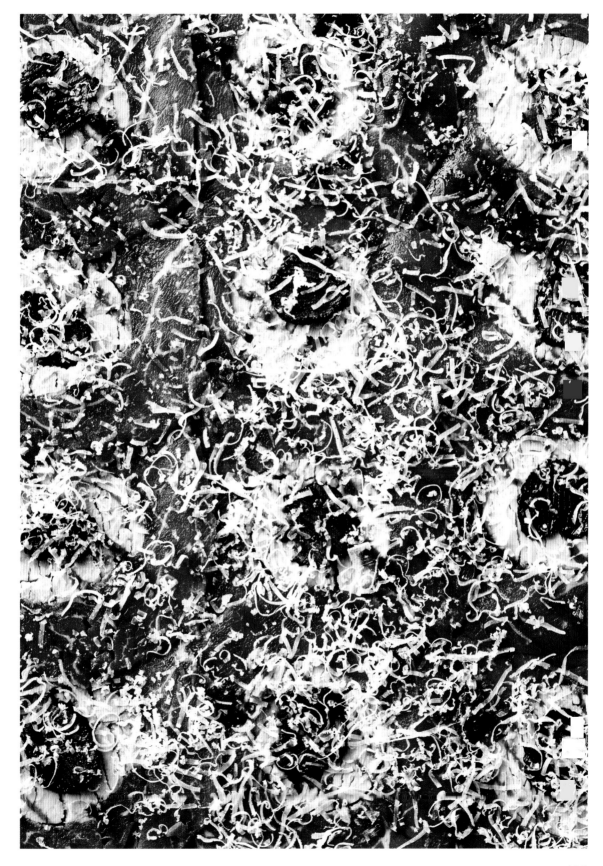

Makes: 15

Preparation time: 3 hours, plus cooling and chilling

Cooking time: 3½ hours

For the apricot jam

500g apricot purée

50g caster sugar

2 cardamom pods, bruised

For the doughnut dough

100g caster sugar

10g instant dried yeast

75ml water

750g plain flour

120g butter, softened

375ml milk

vegetable oil, for deep-frying

For the braised ox cheek

olive oil

2 ox cheeks, trimmed

1 onion, cut into 2cm pieces

1 carrot, cut into 2cm pieces

1 stick of celery, cut into 2cm pieces

2 garlic cloves, crushed

1 glass of red wine

400ml Chicken Stock (see page 216)

1 bay leaf

1 sprig of fresh rosemary

1 sprig of fresh thyme

For the ox cheek filling

500g braised ox cheek, shredded

100g aji panca paste

¼ of a bunch of fresh coriander, chopped

¼ of a bunch of fresh mint, chopped

150g cream cheese

200g Sriracha hot sauce

sea salt and freshly ground black pepper

For the smoked paprika sugar

4 tablespoons caster sugar

1 teaspoon smoked paprika

You will also need a deep-fat fryer

This is one of the dishes that got people talking, but not everyone loves it – it's a bit like Marmite, I guess. It was awarded the number 1 reason to eat out by *Waitrose Kitchen* magazine, which was a great achievement for our humble little doughnut, and one we are all very proud of. We make a spicy filling with slow-braised ox cheek, mix it with cream cheese and various herbs and spices; then, in true doughnut style, we roll them in sugar. But not just any sugar – smoked paprika sugar.

Spicy Ox Cheek Doughnuts with Apricot Jam

To make the apricot jam, put everything in a small saucepan over a medium heat and cook for 20 minutes, or until it becomes a jam-like consistency. Discard the cardamom pods and leave the jam to cool before serving. Keep in the fridge for up to 1 week.

To make the dough, mix the sugar and yeast in a bowl with the water and set aside for 10 minutes. Rub the flour and butter together, then add the yeast mix and the milk and knead for 5 minutes. Put the dough into a clean bowl, cover and refrigerate for 30 minutes–1 hour to firm up.

Preheat your oven to 160°C/gas mark 3.

Heat a drizzle of olive oil in a frying pan and seal the ox cheeks until brown. Transfer them to an ovenproof casserole dish. Add the onion, carrot, celery and garlic to the frying pan and cook gently until tender, with a little colour. Add the wine and simmer until reduced by three-quarters, then pour the contents of the frying pan over the ox cheeks. Add the chicken stock and herbs. Put the lid on the casserole and place in the oven for approximately 3 hours, or until the cheeks give way when pressed with a spoon. Allow to cool in the stock, and when hot enough to handle, take out and break down the meat by shredding with your fingers.

To prepare the ox cheek filling, mix all the ingredients together. Roll into golfball-size balls and refrigerate for 30 minutes to firm up again.

Remove the dough from the fridge. To make a doughnut, take 90g of the dough and flatten it out, then put a ball of the ox cheek mix in the middle and wrap the dough around. Make all the doughnuts this way, then put them into the fridge to rest for 30 minutes.

When ready to cook, heat the vegetable oil to 170°C in your deep-fat fryer. Take the doughnuts out of the fridge and make sure they are completely sealed all the way round. Leave on the side for 10 minutes to prove a little, then cook in batches for 10 minutes, turning them over after 5 minutes, until dark golden.

Mix the sugar and paprika together, and when the doughnuts are cooked roll them in the sugar mix just before serving. Serve with the apricot jam.

I love using mutton, and so should a lot more people. It's great for the farming industry, which needs all the help it can get. Mutton has a reputation for being tough, but that's really not the case – it's just like lamb but with a more intense, grown-up flavour. These sliders are incredibly popular at the restaurant, and you can make them as big or as small as you like. Feel free to add some gem leaves if you like, along with some whole leaves of mint and coriander, and a few ultra-thin slices of red onion, especially if making them normal burger size.

Harissa-spiced Mutton Slider with Lime Crème Fraîche

Makes: 12

Preparation time: 30 minutes, plus cooling

Cooking time: 1½ hours

12 slider-sized burger buns, approximately 5cm wide

Charred Tomato Jam (see page 94)

For the sliders

1 teaspoon olive oil or vegetable oil

1 onion, finely chopped

1 garlic clove, finely chopped

50g harissa paste

1 red chilli, deseeded and finely chopped

1 teaspoon smoked paprika

500g minced mutton (or lamb)

1 sprig of fresh coriander, chopped

1 sprig of fresh mint, chopped

For the lime crème fraîche

4 tablespoons crème fraîche

juice of ½ a lime

finely grated zest of 1 lime

To make the sliders, heat the oil in a frying pan and sweat the onion and garlic gently for 8–10 minutes, or until soft but with no colour. Add the harissa, chilli and paprika and cook for a further 5 minutes. Allow to cool, then put into a bowl, add the minced mutton and herbs, and mix well. Shape the mixture into 12 small patties approximately 5cm wide and 2cm thick and refrigerate until ready to cook.

To make the lime crème fraîche, mix the ingredients together and refrigerate.

When ready to serve, heat a griddle or a frying pan over a high heat and cook the patties for 2–3 minutes on each side.

Split and lightly toast the buns, then add a teaspoon of crème fraîche on one side and a teaspoon of tomato jam on the other. Add the patties and serve.

This is perfect for an afternoon snack, or as something you can eat when you get home after a night out. The chutney recipe came from my time at the Old Brewery in Greenwich, where we used beer in a lot of our dishes, whether it be cooking with the different styles or using the actual ingredients – hops, barley, even recycling the yeast that is skimmed from the top of the tanks.

Rabbit Rillettes with Beer Chutney

Serves: 6
Preparation time: 1 day
Cooking time: 3 hours

For the rillettes

450g rabbit legs
(approximately 2 legs)

2 tablespoons sea salt

1 sprig of fresh rosemary

1 sprig of fresh thyme

500g duck fat (or enough to cover), melted

225g cream cheese

100g butter, softened

65g Dijon mustard

For the beer chutney

360g apples (approximately 3–4 apples), peeled, cored and cut into 1cm pieces

125g raisins

1 onion, finely chopped

1 tablespoon mustard seeds

1 tablespoon ground ginger

125ml white wine vinegar

125ml porter

175g light muscovado sugar

To serve

sourdough bread, toasted

30g pistachios, roasted and crushed

To make the rillettes, put the rabbit legs into a dish. Mix the salt and herbs together and sprinkle all over the rabbit. Cover and leave in the fridge overnight.

When ready to cook, preheat your oven to 130°C/gas mark ½.

Brush off the salt from the rabbit, and place the legs in an ovenproof casserole dish. Add the duck fat and place in the oven for approximately 3 hours, or until the meat falls off the bone. Remove from the oven and allow to cool in the fat.

Remove the legs from the fat, and pick the meat from the bones. Put it into a fresh bowl, add the cream cheese, butter and mustard, and beat together, mixing really well.

To make the chutney, put the apples, raisins, onion, mustard seeds and ginger into a large saucepan and cook gently until soft. Add the vinegar, beer and sugar, lower the heat and cook for approximately 2–3 hours, or until all is reduced and shiny.

Serve the rillettes spread on toast, with the chutney on top and some pistachios sprinkled over.

After testing various marinades for lamb and mutton, Adi, one of our managers, described what we came up with as 'Hara bhara', which translates to 'fresh and green' in Hindi. I love that description, so we called it that on the menu. It's a very herby marinade with a subtle spice, which works really well with the smoky aubergine and is nicely cut by the yoghurt.

Hara Bhara Lamb with Smoky Aubergine and Mint Yoghurt

Serves: 4
Preparation time: 1 day
Cooking time: 1½ hours

8 lamb cutlets

3 aubergines

4 cloves of Confit Garlic (see page 217)

1 teaspoon cumin seeds, toasted

1 sprig of fresh thyme

sea salt and freshly ground black pepper

5 tablespoons organic natural yoghurt

10 fresh mint leaves, finely chopped

For the marinade

¼ of a bunch of fresh coriander

¼ of a bunch of fresh mint

a large pinch of fresh parsley

2 jalapeño chillies

a 5mm piece of fresh ginger

grated zest of ¼ of a lemon

½ teaspoon ground coriander

½ teaspoon ground cumin

seeds from 2 cardamom pods

approximately 50ml olive oil

For the lamb marinade, place all the ingredients except the olive oil in a food processor and pulse, adding the oil in small quantities at a time, until a pesto-like paste is formed. Massage the paste into the lamb cutlets and leave to marinate overnight.

When ready to cook, preheat your oven to 180°C/gas mark 4.

Heat a griddle pan and when hot, add the whole aubergines and char all over until almost burnt.

Place them in a roasting tray and put into the oven for about 30 minutes, or until soft. Allow to cool, then carefully peel away the skin, keeping only the flesh. Place the flesh in a food processor and add the garlic, cumin, thyme (leaves only), salt and pepper. Blitz until smooth, then transfer the mixture to a saucepan and cook over a very low heat for a further 30 minutes, or until dried out a little.

In the meantime, mix together the yoghurt and mint, season with salt and pepper and set aside.

Take the cutlets out of the marinade and season them. Cook them in a griddle pan over a medium heat for approximately 3 minutes on each side. Serve with the smoky aubergine purée and a dollop of mint yoghurt.

After having a beautiful pine tree on display for Christmas, it seemed a waste to throw it away come January, so I picked all the needles off and dried them out for a few days. We then created a wild venison dish and served it alongside a small pile of the pine needles – these had been set on fire and reduced to embers, which had an amazing aroma. Not only is it a nice bit of theatre, but it makes sense too – Scottish deer in the forest among the pine trees, Christmas, bonfires... If you don't have a real pine tree, try using rosemary, which works great too.

Venison Carpaccio with Pear, Almonds and Pine Embers

Serves: 6

Preparation time: 30 minutes (3 hours if drying the rosemary)

Cooking time: none

400g venison fillet steak, trimmed

1 ripe Conference pear, peeled and cut into 1cm dice

1 tablespoon Confit Shallots (see page 217)

20 whole almonds, roasted and crushed

100ml olive oil

30ml sherry vinegar

1 sprig of fresh coriander, chopped

sea salt and freshly ground black pepper

dried pine needles, or rosemary dried in a low or just-used oven for a few hours

Slice the venison as thinly as possible. Arrange the slices over one side of a serving dish, leaving the other side empty for the pine needles.

Put the pear, confit shallots, almonds, olive oil, sherry vinegar and coriander into a bowl and mix together. Season with salt and pepper, then spoon over the carpaccio.

On the other side of the serving dish add a little pile of pine needles. When ready to serve, use a lighter to set the pine needles on fire. The flame will disappear after a few seconds and will then produce a wonderful aroma.

This is what I call beer food, perfect with a chilled lager on a Sunday afternoon; the chicken necks can be prepped well in advance. Best to ask your butcher for these, as most supermarkets won't have them. An amazing snack that costs very little.

Crispy Chicken Necks with Chilli and Garlic

Makes: enough for 4 snacks
Preparation time: 1 day
Cooking time: 1¼ hours

500g chicken necks
¼ of a bunch of fresh parsley
¼ of a bunch of fresh thyme
¼ of a bunch of fresh rosemary
120g caster sugar
120g salt
duck fat, to cover
vegetable oil, for deep-frying
plain flour, for dusting

To serve

¼ teaspoon chilli flakes
2 cloves of Confit Garlic
(see page 217)
sea salt and freshly ground
black pepper
a pinch of chopped fresh parsley
a pinch of chopped fresh chives
a squeeze of lemon juice

You will also need a deep-fat fryer

The day before you want to make these, put the chicken necks into a bowl. Finely chop the parsley, thyme and rosemary and mix with the sugar and salt. Sprinkle all over the chicken necks, then cover and refrigerate overnight.

When ready to cook, preheat your oven to 130°C/gas mark ½.

Remove the chicken necks from the marinade and place them in an ovenproof casserole dish. Cover them with duck fat and place in the oven for about 1½ hours, or until the meat on the necks pulls away from the bone. Allow to cool in the fat, then take the necks out of the fat and refrigerate if not eating right away.

When ready to cook, heat the oil to 180°C in your deep-fat fryer. Lightly dust the necks with flour, then fry in batches for about 3 minutes, or until crisp. Drain on kitchen paper.

Put the chilli flakes, confit garlic, seasoning and herbs into a bowl and mix gently with a spoon so that the garlic cloves break up a little.

Remove the necks from the deep-fat fryer, add to the seasoning bowl and mix well. Finish with a squeeze of lemon and eat straight away.

Serves: 6

Preparation time: 1 day

Cooking time: 4½ hours

4 Barbecued Spiced Pig's Ears
(see page 194)

100g plain flour

2 eggs, beaten

100g breadcrumbs

vegetable oil, for deep-frying

sea salt and freshly ground
black pepper

½ a lemon

1 recipe Spice Mix (see page 194)

For the pig's cheek nuggets

8 pig's cheeks, trimmed

olive oil

½ an onion, cut into 2cm pieces

½ a carrot, cut into 2cm pieces

1 stick of celery, cut into 2cm pieces

2 garlic cloves, crushed

1 sprig of fresh thyme

1 sprig of fresh rosemary

1 bay leaf

1 glass of red wine

750ml Chicken Stock
see page 216)

50g Parmesan cheese, grated

1 sprig of fresh parsley, chopped

1 tablespoon Confit Shallots
(see page 217)

For the pig's tails

6 pig's tails

½ an onion, cut into 2cm pieces

½ a carrot, cut into 2cm pieces

1 stick of celery, cut into 2cm pieces

2 garlic cloves, crushed

1 sprig of fresh thyme

1 sprig of fresh rosemary

1 bay leaf

1 glass of red wine

750ml Chicken Stock
(see page 216)

You will also need a deep-fat fryer

Inspired by the traditional fritto misto from Italy, this is my take on it, but porkified. A great dish for a night in front of the TV, or a starter for the table to get stuck into, it's cheap and fun to see how tasty these forgotten cuts can be. You can even throw in a few 'quavers' from page 199...

Piggy Fritto Misto

Follow the Day 1 method for the pig's ears on page 194.

For the pig's cheek nuggets, heat a drizzle of olive oil in a frying pan and sear the pig's cheeks until golden brown. Place the cheeks in a saucepan. Add the onion, carrot, celery and garlic to the frying pan and cook gently for about 5 minutes. Add to the cheeks, with the thyme, rosemary and bay leaf. Deglaze the pan with the red wine, and simmer until reduced by half. Pour over the cheeks, and cover with the chicken stock. Cook over a low heat for approximately 4 hours, or until the cheeks are tender and break down very easily when squeezed. Allow to cool in the stock.

Meanwhile, cook the pig's tails: Preheat the oven to 120°C/gas mark ½. Place all the pig's tails ingredients in an ovenproof casserole dish, cover with foil and place in the oven for approximately 3 hours, or until the meat gives when squeezed. Allow to cool in the stock, as with the cheeks, and when cool take out, drain and refrigerate. When chilled, dust with half the flour, roll in one of the beaten eggs and coat with half breadcrumbs, then set aside for later.

When cool, remove the pig's cheeks from the stock and flake into a mixing bowl. Strain the stock into another saucepan and simmer until reduced to a glaze with a consistency like honey. Add to the flaked cheeks and mix well. Add the Parmesan, parsley and confit shallots and mix well. Roll into grape-size balls and place in the fridge to firm up. When firm, dust with the remaining flour, roll in the remaining beaten egg and coat with rest of the breadcrumbs, then set aside for later.

When ready to eat, heat the oil to 180°C in your deep-fat fryer and dust the pig's ears with flour. Fry the tails first for about 6 minutes, or until golden brown and hot inside, then drain on kitchen paper. Next fry the ears and nuggets for 3–4 minutes. Drain well and place everything on a serving plate.

Season the tails and nuggets with salt and a squeeze of lemon juice, and for the ears use the spice mix on page 194 to season separately.

Makes: 8

Preparation time: 2 hours

Cooking time: 45 minutes

500g puff pastry

plain flour, for dusting

eggwash (2 eggs beaten with
50ml milk)

For the sausage mix

200g Middle White pork
(or any other rare breed pork
you can get), minced

100g foie gras, deveined
and cut into 1cm cubes

2 Cumberland sausages,
skins removed

50g breadcrumbs

1 sprig of fresh parsley, chopped

4 tablespoons Confit Shallots
(see page 217)

4 cloves of Confit Garlic
(see page 217)

1 sprig of fresh thyme, leaves only

8 Agen prunes, soaked in brandy
overnight and chopped into
1cm pieces

sea salt and freshly ground
black pepper

For the lentils

olive oil

1 onion, finely chopped

1 stick of celery, finely chopped

1 carrot, finely chopped

1 sprig of fresh thyme

200g Puy lentils

500ml Chicken Stock
(see page 216)

2 sprigs of fresh parsley,
finely chopped

50ml sherry vinegar

20g butter

20g plain flour

Being English, sausage rolls have always been a part of my life since I was a kid, and it was only a matter of time before I started playing with them. This is a recipe I started cooking back in 2008 at the Ambassador, which went down really well with our guests.

Middle White Pork Sausage Rolls with Prunes and Lentils

First, make the sausage mixture. Mix all ingredients together and season with salt and pepper.

On a floured surface, roll out the pastry 2mm thick and cut it into 8 rectangles, each 15 x 10cm. Take one rectangle at a time, and on one half spoon the mixture in a sausage-like line down the longer side. Eggwash all around, then fold over the pastry and seal with a fork. Put on a baking tray lined with baking paper, and make 3 cuts in the top for the steam to escape. Refrigerate for at least 30 minutes to firm up the pastry.

Preheat your oven to 180°C/gas mark 4.

For the lentils, heat a splash of olive oil in a saucepan over a medium heat. Add the onion, celery, carrot and thyme, and cook gently without colouring. Add the lentils and the stock and simmer for approximately 20 minutes, or until the lentils are cooked. Add the parsley and sherry vinegar and season with salt and pepper.

Mix the butter and flour together to form a paste, roll it into small balls and drop them into the lentils. Turn the heat up and mix well. As the butter and flour melt, the mixture will begin to thicken. Cook for a further 5 minutes.

Take the tray of sausage rolls out of the fridge and eggwash the tops and sides. Place them in the middle of the oven and cook for about 20–25 minutes, or until golden brown. Serve in bowls, with the lentils on the bottom and the sausage rolls on top.

Back in the days when everyone had fires roaring in the winter, and the mist and fog of the Thames Valley combined with the smoke, the result was often referred to as a pea souper, which later became London Particular. Nowadays, the idiom is reversed and we call pea and ham soup 'London Particular'. Peas and ham, ham and eggs – both present themselves as obvious garnishes, so we use both for this winter warmer.

London Particular

Serves: 8

Preparation time: 30 minutes, plus cooling

Cooking time: 4 hours

500g dried split peas (follow packet instructions for soaking)

1 smoked ham hock

1 onion, peeled and left whole

2 sticks of celery, chopped

1 bay leaf

1 sprig of fresh thyme

sea salt and freshly ground black pepper

vegetable oil, for frying

8 slow-cooked eggs (see page 86) or regular poached eggs

plain flour, for dusting

2 handfuls of pea shoots

6 fresh mint leaves, finely sliced

Put the split peas, ham hock, onion, celery, bay leaf and thyme into a large saucepan and add water to cover. Bring to the boil, then lower the heat and cook for approximately 3½ hours, skimming regularly, until the meat comes away from the bone of the ham hock. The peas may catch on the bottom, so stir frequently and top up with water as necessary. The final consistency should be that of a thick soup.

Remove the ham hock and allow to cool. In the meantime, remove the bay leaf and thyme and discard, then blitz the soup in a food processor until smooth. Correct the seasoning. When the ham hock is cool, take the meat off the bone and flake it into small strands. Pat dry with kitchen paper.

Heat the oil to 180°C in your deep-fat fryer or in a heavy-based saucepan.

Bring a saucepan of water to the boil. Either reheat your slow-cooked eggs or poach your eggs traditionally in the water. Meanwhile, gently reheat your soup.

Dust a handful of the ham flakes with flour and fry until crisp (this should only take 2 minutes), then drain and set aside for garnishing.

Put some of the flaked ham in the bottom of each serving bowl, about a tablespoon per person. Fill the bowl with soup, put an egg on top and season with salt and pepper. Garnish with the pea shoots, finely sliced mint leaves and the crispy ham.

Serves: 4

Preparation time: 1 hour,
plus resting

Cooking time: 2 hours

For the endive marmalade

2 tablespoons vegetable oil

4 heads of red endive, sliced into matchstick-size pieces

1 onion, finely sliced

2 cloves of Confit Garlic
(see page 217)

½ a glass of red wine

½ a glass of port

grated zest and juice of 3 oranges

1 sprig of fresh thyme

1 sprig of fresh rosemary

2 tablespoons caster sugar

1 star anise

sea salt and freshly ground
black pepper

juice of 3 oranges

70ml walnut oil

2 onions, peeled and halved

3 garlic cloves, crushed but
unpeeled

2 carrots, peeled and halved
lengthways

2 bay leaves

1 sprig of fresh thyme

2 sprigs of fresh sage

500g piece of pork belly, scored

olive oil

400ml Chicken Stock
(see page 216)

12 walnut halves, roasted

watercress, to garnish

I absolutely adore pig in any form, but pork belly remains king; so juicy and tender. This is served with a bittersweet endive marmalade, which cuts the fat nicely. Very much a small plate – you can tweak the dish and add creamy mash and maybe some sprouting broccoli, but keep the marmalade or it could become too rich.

Crispy Pork Belly with Endive Marmalade, Orange and Walnuts

To make the endive marmalade, heat the vegetable oil in a large saucepan. Add the endive, onion and garlic and cook gently until soft and lightly coloured.

Put the red wine, port, orange zest and juice, thyme, rosemary, sugar and star anise into another saucepan and bring to the boil, then lower the heat and simmer for 15 minutes to infuse the flavours. Strain, then pour the liquid into the pan of endive and onion and turn the heat to medium. Season with salt and pepper and cook slowly for about 45 minutes, or until the mixture has reduced to the consistency of a jam.

Put the orange juice into a small saucepan and bring to the boil, then lower the heat and simmer until it has reduced by about three-quarters and is almost a caramel. Gradually whisk in the walnut oil until it emulsifies, then set aside for later.

To cook the pork belly, preheat your oven to 200°C/gas mark 6.

Put the onions, garlic, carrots and herbs into a roasting tray. Put the pork joint on top, drizzle with olive oil and season well. Roast in the oven for about 30 minutes, or until the crackling begins to form, at which point reduce the temperature to 150°C/gas mark 2. Add the stock and continue roasting for another hour or so, then remove from the oven and let the pork rest for 30 minutes.

Slice off the skin of the pork, and if it is not crisp, pop it back in the oven for 10 minutes or so. If it is crisp, slice it into 1cm strips. Strain the liquid from the roasting tray and reserve.

Carve each person a nice slice of pork, and serve with a spoonful of marmalade, a few walnuts crushed over and a couple of slices of crackling. Finish with a spoonful of the roasting juices and some watercress, dressed with the orange and walnut emulsion.

This dish, while a tad tricky to prepare, has a great wow factor. We remove the bones from the fish, leaving the head and tail intact, with the belly left in, so the fish is used as a basket for the fresh summer vegetables to sit inside. At the restaurant, as the seasons change, we adapt the garnish, using ingredients such as wild mushrooms, Jerusalem artichokes, asparagus and wild garlic.

Whole Baked Sea Bass with Courgettes, Baby Potatoes and Peas

Serves: 2

Preparation time: 45 minutes

Cooking time: 1 hour

1 sea bass (approximately 1kg), left whole, scaled (try asking your fishmonger to 'canoe cut' – or see the method below)

olive oil

sea salt and freshly ground black pepper

100g butter

10 new potatoes, cooked and skins removed

100g shelled fresh peas, blanched and refreshed

2 courgettes, diced, blanched and refreshed

200ml Chicken Stock (see page 216)

10 fresh mint leaves, finely chopped

2 plum tomatoes, peeled, deseeded and cut into 1cm cubes

watercress or pea shoots, to garnish

½ a lemon

If preparing the fish yourself, fillet it from the back down, but don't cut through the stomach cavity. When completed on both sides, take a pair of scissors and snip the bone behind the head and at the tail, so you can remove all the bones. Take out all the guts, and remove the bloodline, fins and gills. Give the fish a really good wash. Pat dry with kitchen paper, and pin-bone.

Preheat your oven to 180°C/gas mark 4. Place the fish on a baking tray lined with oiled baking paper, belly down, with the fillets opened out. Drizzle with olive oil, season with salt and pepper and place in the oven – it should take about 10–15 minutes to cook.

In the meantime, heat the butter in a large frying pan. When foaming, add the potatoes, peas and courgettes and give them a good sauté. Season, then slowly add the chicken stock, 1 ladle at a time, allowing it to reduce before adding more. At the end you should have a buttery, emulsified sauce around the vegetables. Finish with the mint and chopped tomatoes.

Remove the fish from the oven, and carefully lift it off the tray with a palette knife, on to a serving dish. Pour the vegetables into the cavity of the fish. Garnish with some watercress or pea shoots if you like, and squeeze over the lemon.

Use whatever fish is fresh and at its best on the day – the ones I've listed below are great, but are only an example. Monkfish, pollock, mackerel and sea bream are all good. If you can find them, garnish with any sea vegetables – samphire, sea rosemary, sea purslane – you can get your hands on.

Seared Dayboat Fish Stew with Spring Vegetables

Serves: 4
Preparation time: 20 minutes
Cooking time: 1½ hours

olive oil

1 onion, cut into 1cm dice

2 sticks of celery, cut into 1cm dice

1 leek, cut into 1cm dice

1 sprig of fresh thyme

2 bay leaves

¼ of a bunch of fresh parsley, stalks and leaves separated

1kg fish bones, cleaned and washed

2 glasses of white wine

1.5 litres water

300g mussels

300g clams

20 leaves of fresh chives, cut into 2.5cm batons

100g butter

2 sea bass fillets, each one cut in half

4 pieces of cod, approximately 100g each, skin on

sea salt and freshly ground black pepper

1 bunch of baby carrots, trimmed, blanched and refreshed

1 bunch of baby turnips, trimmed, blanched and refreshed

1 bunch of baby leeks, trimmed, blanched and refreshed

Heat a little olive oil in a large saucepan and add the onion, celery, leek, thyme, bay leaves and parsley stalks. Cook gently for 10–12 minutes, or until softened but with no colour, then add the fish bones and cook for a further 10 minutes.

Add the wine and cook until reduced by three-quarters. Add about 1.5 litres of cold water, or enough to cover, then bring to the boil. Lower the heat and simmer for 30 minutes, skimming frequently. Strain as much veg and fish as possible, then put the broth back into the saucepan and simmer until reduced by half.

When ready to eat, heat the broth and add the mussels, clams, parsley leaves and chives. Add the butter and allow it to melt and enrich the broth.

Heat a little olive oil in a frying pan. Season the sea bass and cod with salt and pepper, add to the pan and cook, skin side down, or until the skin is crisp.

Add the blanched vegetables to the broth, and allow to reheat for 3–4 minutes. Discard any mussels and clams that remain closed. Pour the stew into a large serving bowl, and place the seared fish on top. Garnish with sea vegetables, if you have them.

Salt-baking is a great technique, with both theatre and impressive results. While the salt bakes it comes together to form a thick crust, so that as the fish bakes the steam that's released, rather than escaping, is absorbed back into the fish, keeping it juicy. The aromats release all their beautiful flavours, so your kitchen will smell amazing – the ones we use are just a guideline – you can use whatever tickles your fancy. Use whatever vegetables are in season, and if you can't find dried seaweed use a selection of fresh soft herbs instead.

Salt-baked Sea Bream with Market Vegetables and Seaweed Butter Sauce

Serves: 2

Preparation time: 20 minutes

Cooking time: 40 minutes

seeds from 2 cardamom pods

a pinch of fennel seeds

a pinch of fenugreek seeds

a pinch of coriander seeds

10 juniper berries

2 star anise

2 cloves

200g sea salt

2 egg whites, beaten until stiff

1 whole sea bream, scaled and gutted, fins and gills removed

olive oil

1 shallot, finely chopped

finely grated zest and juice of 2 lemons

100g butter, cubed

sea salt and freshly ground black pepper

a pinch of dried Irish sea dulse, rehydrated and finely chopped

2 heads of baby fennel, blanched and refreshed

1 bunch of baby leeks, blanched and refreshed

1 bunch of baby carrots, blanched and refreshed

Preheat your oven to 180°C/gas mark 4.

To make the salt crust, mix all the spices together in a bowl, then add the salt and the whisked egg white and fold in to form a paste. Place your sea bream on a lightly oiled baking sheet lined with baking paper and spread the salt crust over the skin, leaving the head and tail exposed. The crust should be about 2–3cm thick. Bake in the oven for approximately 25–30 minutes. To tell if it is ready, insert a flat-edged knife into the thickest part of the fish – after a few seconds remove the knife and the blade should feel hot to touch.

Meanwhile, heat a little olive oil in a frying pan and cook the shallot gently until soft. Add the lemon juice and cook until reduced by half, then slowly add the butter, in small knobs, whisking as you go so that the sauce emulsifies. Season with salt and pepper, then add the lemon zest and seaweed (or herbs, see introduction) and give it a good stir. Set aside and keep warm.

When ready to serve, reheat your vegetables and the sauce and season with salt and pepper. Remove the fish from the oven, and allow to rest for 5 minutes. Slide the fish on to a serving dish and take to the table. Carefully lift off the salt crust and discard. Remove and discard the skin from the fish and serve with the vegetables, and the sauce in a jug on the side.

Another example of mixing cured pork with shellfish, and one that can be easily modified to make a soup. If wild garlic isn't in season, try adding a clove or two of confit garlic at the end (see page 217), and add some parsley in place of the wild garlic leaves.

Baked Cod with Clam Chowder and Bacon

Serves: 2

Preparation time: 20 minutes

Cooking time: 1 hour 15 minutes

8 rashers of smoked streaky bacon, finely sliced into 2mm lardons

1 onion, finely diced

1 garlic clove, finely diced

1 sprig of fresh thyme

1 bay leaf

200ml double cream

200ml Chicken Stock (see page 216)

2 potatoes, peeled and cut into 1cm dice

2 portions of cod, approximately 160g each, skin on

olive oil

sea salt and freshly ground black pepper

4 wild garlic leaves, cut into 2cm pieces

For the clams

300g clams

1 glass of white wine

1 shallot, diced

1 garlic clove, crushed

1 sprig of fresh thyme

First, cook the clams. Put the clams, white wine, shallot, garlic and thyme into a mixing bowl. Heat a medium saucepan, and when it's hot, tip in the contents of the bowl and cover immediately. After 2–3 minutes the clams will open, at which point take the pan off the heat and strain. Discard any clams that don't open. Pass the stock through a fine sieve, or, better still, a clean tea towel, to remove any dirt, as the stock will be used for the chowder. Pick the meat out of most of the clam shells, saving a few in the shell for a garnish.

Preheat your oven to 180°C/gas mark 4.

Heat a medium saucepan and add the bacon. Cook gently until golden brown, pouring away any fat that comes out. Keep scraping the bottom of the pan – that's where all the flavour is. Add the onion, garlic, thyme and bay leaf and cook gently until soft.

Now add the clam stock and simmer until reduced by three-quarters. Add the cream, chicken stock and diced potatoes and cook for about 20 minutes, or until the potatoes are cooked. Keep an eye that it doesn't catch.

Put the cod on a baking sheet lined with baking paper, drizzle with olive oil and season with salt and pepper. Bake in the oven for about 8–10 minutes, or until just cooked through.

To serve, remove the thyme and bay leaf from the chowder, add the clams and the wild garlic, or, if using, confit garlic and herbs (see introduction), and allow to cook for a few minutes. Taste and correct the seasoning at this stage.

Serve in large bowls with the cod, seasoned with salt and pepper on top, with the clams in the shell in full view.

Being such a robust fish, monkfish goes great with earthy flavours such as wild mushrooms, Jerusalem artichokes and salsify. This dish is perfect for autumn, and the addition of smoked butter really brings the ingredients together. If you can't get hold of trompette mushrooms, mixed wild mushrooms are fine. Pancetta would work well here too – food for thought...

Roast Monkfish with Salsify and Jerusalem Artichokes

Serves: 2

Preparation time: 20 minutes

Cooking time: 45 minutes

vegetable oil, for deep-frying

1 handful of Jerusalem artichokes, peeled and cut into 2cm slices

2 sticks of salsify, peeled and sliced into 2cm pieces on the angle

sea salt and freshly ground black pepper

juice of ½ a lemon

olive oil

2 portions of monkfish, approximately 200g each, on the bone, membrane removed

100g butter, plus a little for the fish

2 sprigs of fresh thyme

a dash of liquid smoke

100g trompette mushrooms, washed

300ml Chicken Stock (see page 216)

1 sprig of fresh parsley, finely chopped

To garnish

2 Jerusalem artichokes, cut into paper-thin slices

Heat the vegetable oil to 180°C in a deep-fat fryer, or in a deep heavy-based saucepan.

Put the artichokes and salsify into a saucepan, cover with cold water and add salt and a squeeze of lemon juice to help keep them nice and white. Bring to the boil, then lower the heat and simmer gently until a knife goes through with a little resistance.

Carefully lower the sliced artichokes for the garnish into the hot oil in batches, and deep-fry for 1–2 minutes, or until golden brown like crisps. Remove, drain on kitchen paper and season with salt and pepper.

Preheat your oven to 180°C/gas mark 4.

Heat a little olive oil in a frying pan. Season the monkfish, add to the pan and cook on both sides to seal. Place the pieces of fish on a baking sheet lined with baking paper and put a small knob of butter and a sprig of thyme on top of each one, then put into the oven for about 10–15 minutes, or until cooked through.

Allow the butter to soften, and then beat in the liquid smoke until you have the desired taste, mixing well. Put into the fridge to firm up a little.

Melt the smoked butter in a frying pan, then add the artichokes, salsify and mushrooms and sauté until caramelized. Gradually add the chicken stock, allowing it to reduce after each addition to create a rich butter sauce around the vegetables. This should take around 10 minutes. Season with salt and pepper and the chopped parsley.

After 15 minutes the fish should be ready. Remove from the oven and let it rest for 5 minutes. Serve the vegetables in a bowl, with the fish sitting on top and the Jerusalem artichoke crisps sprinkled around.

Tom came up with this idea, and it's typical of his style: fresh, simple and downright tasty. Mackerel, when fresh out of the water, is hard to beat. Such beautiful colours in the skin, and the deep, earthy flavour goes really well with the smoky bacon and fresh minted peas.

Cornish Mackerel with Split Peas, Mint and Bacon

Serves: 2

Preparation time: 30 minutes, plus soaking

Cooking time: 1½ hours

100g split green peas (follow packet instructions for soaking)

½ an onion, left in one piece

1 small stick of celery

1 bay leaf

1 sprig of fresh thyme

350–500ml Chicken Stock (see page 216)

sea salt and freshly ground black pepper

4 rashers of smoked streaky bacon, cut into 1cm lardons

2 slices of sourdough bread, cut into 1cm dice

olive oil, for frying

4 fresh mackerel fillets, pin-boned

6 fresh mint leaves, roughly chopped

2 handfuls of pea shoots

30ml Sherry Dressing (see page 216)

First, drain your soaked peas. Give them a good wash and put them into a medium saucepan. Add the onion, celery, bay leaf and thyme, and enough chicken stock to cover. Season with salt and pepper, bring to the boil, then lower the heat and cook gently at a simmer, using the rest of the chicken stock to top up when necessary – they should be cooked in about 45–50 minutes.

Put the bacon into a frying pan over a medium heat and cook to release the fat. When the bacon starts to colour, add the diced bread and let it fry in the bacon fat until it becomes crunchy. Set aside if not using right away.

When ready to serve, heat another frying pan and add a drizzle of olive oil. Season the mackerel fillets on both sides and add them to the pan, skin side down. They may contract a little, but don't worry, just gently press them back down for a few seconds and they will relax back to normal. Sear over a medium heat for about 4 minutes, or until crisp and golden brown. At this point they will almost be cooked through, but turn each one over and allow the flesh to finish cooking through.

Fold the mint into the split peas and place in the bottom of each serving bowl. Put the mackerel fillets on top, then a good spoonful of the bacon and bread mix. Finally, garnish with the pea shoots and drizzle with the sherry dressing.

Serves: 4

Preparation time: 1 hour

Cooking time: 2 hours

For the sage and onion stuffing

100g butter

1 onion, finely diced

1 garlic clove, finely diced

sea salt and freshly ground black pepper

2 sprigs of fresh sage

1 handful of mixed wild mushrooms, roughly chopped

120g sourdough bread, crusts removed, cut into 1cm dice

1 handful of ready-cooked chestnuts, crushed

2 eggs

3 Cumberland sausages, skin removed

For the chicken

1 large whole chicken, plump, organic or free-range

1 onion, peeled and halved

1 head of garlic, halved horizontally

2 sprigs of fresh thyme

1 sprig of fresh rosemary

1 sprig of fresh sage, finely chopped

olive oil

1 litre Chicken Stock (see page 216)

For the roast potatoes

3 tablespoons duck fat

8 Maris Piper potatoes, peeled and halved

1 sprig of fresh rosemary

1 sprig of fresh thyme

3 garlic cloves, unpeeled

For the chicken skin gravy

100g chicken skins

olive oil

2 shallots, sliced

1 sprig of fresh thyme

It goes without saying that a Sunday roast is my all-time favourite meal. Whether it's after football as a kid, or after a long week at work, nothing can soothe your pains like a good roast. It's something every family should do on a Sunday – invite friends, colleagues, whoever, just roast some meat and eat it together, with enough roasties to induce a food coma. Use whatever veggies are in season: parsnips and spring greens, mashed swede, sprouting broccoli, buttered carrots – the list goes on...

Sunday Chicken

First, make the stuffing. Melt the butter in a frying pan and cook the onion and garlic until soft. Season with salt and pepper. Add the sage and the mushrooms, and continue to cook until soft and translucent. Add the bread and allow to soak up any butter, then transfer to a mixing bowl. Add the chestnuts and give it all a good mix. Allow to cool, then add the eggs and sausage meat and mix well. Set aside in the fridge.

Preheat your oven to 180°C/gas mark 4. Make sure all the guts are removed from the chicken and fill the cavity with the stuffing. If there's any stuffing left over, you can either freeze it for next time, or roll it into balls and bake it separately.

Put the onion, garlic and herbs into a roasting tray. Place the chicken on top, and drizzle with olive oil. Season well and place in the oven. After about 40 minutes the chicken will be nice and brown – at this point add half the stock, then lower the oven temperature to 160°C/gas mark 3 and roast for a further 30 minutes or until cooked.

In the meantime, make your roasties. Place the duck fat in a roasting tray and put it into the oven. Put the potatoes into a saucepan and cover with cold water. Season really well, don't be shy with the salt. Bring the potatoes to the boil, then lower the heat and simmer gently until they are halfway cooked. Strain, and leave them to sit on the side on a tray or plate. Don't shake them, just let the steam escape.

Take the tray of duck fat out of the oven and carefully add the potatoes, taking care not to splash, as you'll burn yourself. Using a spoon, baste each potato with the fat, then put them into the oven. Keep basting every 20 minutes or so, and after the first 30 minutes add the rosemary, thyme and garlic. They should be ready in 1½ hours.

To make the gravy, put the chicken skins into a saucepan with a splash of olive oil over a medium heat and cook gently, stirring frequently, until they begin to colour. Don't worry if they catch a little, just keep scraping the pan, that's where all the flavour is. As the fat is released, pour it away. Once nicely coloured and the fat has been released, add the shallots and thyme, and cook for a further 10 minutes or so.

When the chicken is ready, take it out of the oven and allow to rest for about 30 minutes. Strain the stock from the tray and add to the pan of chicken skin. Add the rest of the stock and turn the heat up high. Reduce rapidly for about 20 minutes, or until you have a gravy consistency. Strain and serve alongside your chicken, carving at the table.

Serves: 4

Preparation time: 1 day

Cooking time: 3 hours, 40 minutes

4 duck legs

100g Duck Cure (see page 218)

500g duck fat, enough to cover the duck legs

oil, for brushing

butter, for frying

4 duck eggs

For the waffle mix

180g plain flour

10g caster sugar

1 teaspoon baking powder

½ teaspoon bicarbonate of soda

a pinch of salt

180ml buttermilk

35g butter, melted

1 small egg

For the maple syrup

200ml maple syrup

25g yellow mustard seeds

1 teaspoon mustard powder

2.5cm piece of cinnamon stick

1 sprig of fresh thyme

You will also need a waffle iron

Timon Balloo, Executive Chef and Partner at Duck & Waffle's sister restaurant Sugarcane in Midtown Miami, created this iconic dish and explains how this dish was born: 'This dish encompasses my upbringing in urban California, eating fried chicken and waffles, and my refined culinary training working with some great French chefs. And the egg part? If I had my way I'd put eggs on top of everything. But in this case it works especially well when you burst the yolk and it oozes into the meat; add a little of the mustard seed maple syrup and it's an awesome balance of sweet and savoury.'

Duck and Waffle with Mustard Maple Syrup

The day before, sprinkle the duck legs all over with the cure. Put them into a container with a lid and leave in the fridge overnight.

The next day, preheat your oven to 140°C/gas mark 1. Take out the duck legs and brush off all of the cure. Place in an ovenproof casserole dish and cover with the duck fat. Put into the oven and cook for approximately 3 hours, or until the meat just falls off the bone. Allow to cool in the fat.

To make the waffle mix, put the flour, sugar, baking powder, bicarbonate of soda and salt into a bowl and whisk together. In another bowl, whisk together the buttermilk, melted butter and egg, then whisk this into the flour mixture until just combined. The mixture will be quite thick, which is perfectly normal. Put into the fridge until you are ready to make your waffles.

Combine all the ingredients for the maple syrup in a saucepan and bring to the boil. Take off the heat and leave to cool for the flavours to infuse. Remove the cinnamon and thyme, but leave the mustard seeds, as they add a nice dimension when bitten into.

When ready to serve, preheat your oven to 180°C/gas mark 4 and turn on your waffle iron. Heat an ovenproof frying pan and add the duck legs, skin side down. Once the skin starts to crisp, turn the legs over and put into the oven for about 8–10 minutes, or until crisp.

While the duck legs are in the oven, make your 4 waffles. Brush the hot waffle iron with oil and pour a ladle of batter into each mould. Spread it all around, as the mix is quite thick and won't spread on its own. Cook for about 3 minutes, or until golden and cooked through.

Put another frying pan on to heat. Melt some butter in the hot pan and gently fry the duck eggs, spooning the hot butter over the yolk right at the end.

Serve a duck leg on top of each waffle, with an egg on top of the duck, and maple syrup on the side. When eating, crack the yolk first, then pour over the syrup, otherwise the syrup tends to slip off the egg.

Nothing says 'for the table' more than a whole roasted ham hock, studded with aromatic cloves and glazed with honey. I love to serve this simply with whatever vegetables are at the market, and with freshly baked bread and loads of butter, but you can try serving it with mashed potatoes or even a root vegetable gratin. In this recipe we use the colourful heritage carrots and an interesting technique of baking turnips in salt. Make sure you save the stock from cooking the ham – it's great in soups and stews for that smoked bacon hit.

Honey-glazed Ham Hock with Carrots and Salt-baked Turnips

Serves: 2–3

Preparation time: 1 hour

Cooking time: 5 hours

1 smoked ham hock

1 onion, halved

1 stick of celery

2 carrots, halved

1 bay leaf

1 sprig of fresh thyme

10 black peppercorns

8 cloves

2 turnips, peeled

2 tablespoons honey

50g butter

6 heritage carrots, blanched (left whole)

sprig of fresh thyme (optional)

1 good handful of watercress

50ml Sherry Dressing (see page 216)

For the salt crust

250g plain flour

150g sea salt

150ml water

Put the ham hock, onion, celery, carrots, bay leaf, thyme and peppercorns into a large saucepan and cover with cold water. Bring to the boil, then lower the heat and simmer and cook for approximately 3–3½ hours, or until the meat comes away from the bone. Make sure you skim all the time, and top up with water when necessary. Allow the ham to cool in the stock, then take out and carefully peel away the leathery skin. Score the fat and evenly stud with the cloves, then place in a roasting dish. Reserve the stock.

Preheat your oven to 180°C/gas mark 4.

To make the salt dough, mix the flour and salt in a bowl, and add the water until you have a firm dough. You may not need to use all the water. Divide in half, then wrap each turnip in the dough so it's totally encased and put them on a roasting tray.

Pour 50ml of the ham stock around the ham hock, then drizzle the honey over the ham and place in the bottom of the oven. Place the turnips in the oven on the middle shelf. Both should take around 30 minutes if the ham hock was at room temperature or hotter. (If you cooked it in advance and refrigerated it, start the hock in the oven 45 minutes before the turnips, at 160°C/gas mark 3, then when you add the turnips increase the heat to 180°C/gas mark 4 – this will give the hock a nice glaze, but keep an eye on it.) Baste the hock with any honey that falls off.

While the ham and turnips are cooking, melt the butter in a frying pan and add your carrots. Slowly cook them so they begin to colour and the butter foams. Feel free to add a sprig of thyme here if you like.

When the hock and turnips are ready, remove them both from the oven. Carefully break off the salt crust from the turnips and discard. Slice the turnips about 5mm thick.

Put the hock, carrots and turnips on a large serving plate, and pour any juice from the ham hock all over and around. Serve with the watercress dressed with the sherry dressing.

Serves: 8–10

Preparation time: 30 minutes, plus soaking

Cooking time: 6 hours

1 cooked ham hock
(cooked according to the recipe
for the ham hock opposite, up to
the stage where you remove the
skin, stock reserved and strained)

For the stuffing

50g butter

50ml olive oil

2 onions, finely diced

2 sticks of celery, finely diced

2 garlic cloves, finely diced

6 fresh sage leaves, roughly sliced

1 handful of mixed wild
mushrooms, cut into 2cm pieces

300g pearl barley (see packet
instructions for soaking)

ham stock (from cooking the ham)
or chicken stock

3 handfuls of ham hock meat,
picked to small pieces

For the suckling pig

1 suckling pig, deboned,
head left on

3 Bramley apples, halved

2 onions, halved

3 carrots, halved

500ml apple juice

500ml Chicken Stock
(see page 216)

200ml maple syrup

50g butter

To garnish

watercress

mixed pickles (apple, carrot, fennel
and/or turnip, see page 216)

This is a real showstopper, a dish created by one of our sous chefs, Jacek. Get it cooking in the early afternoon and your house will be full of the wonderful aromas of suckling pig by the time your friends or family arrive. If you make pickles, make a varied batch so you always have some to hand, using the pickling liquid on page 216. Pickled apple, carrot, fennel and turnip all work well with this, but pretty much anything goes – the idea is to have some acidity to cut the richness.

Slow-roasted Suckling Pig with Mushrooms and Barley

First make the stuffing. Heat the butter and oil in an ovenproof casserole dish, then add the onion, celery, garlic, sage and mushrooms and cook gently until soft and tender. Drain the soaked barley and add to the casserole, stirring to give it a good coat in the butter and oil. Add enough of the ham stock to cover (or chicken stock if you don't have), bring to the boil, then reduce the heat and simmer. Continue to cook and add stock when needed for about 45 minutes, or until the barley is soft and looks like a loose risotto. Mix in the ham hock meat and set aside to cool.

Preheat your oven to 120°C/gas mark ½.

Open out the suckling pig and place the stuffing in the stomach cavity. Roll up and tie with butcher's string.

Put the halved apples, onions and carrots into a large roasting tray and sit the suckling pig on top, bent slightly so it fits snugly, without it touching the tray. Add the apple juice and chicken stock, then cover the whole dish with foil. You may want to cover the ears with an extra layer of foil to avoid burning. Roast in the oven for approximately 4 hours, or until the meat is tender and the skin is soft and sticky.

Gently transfer the suckling pig from the tray into another clean one, and turn the oven up to 160°C/gas mark 3. Pour one third of the maple syrup over the pig and place in the oven. After 20 minutes, pour over half the remaining maple syrup, and pour over the rest after a further 20 minutes for one last glaze.

In the meantime, strain the roasting juices from the first tray into a saucepan (discard the apples, onions and carrots), bring to the boil, then reduce the heat and simmer until reduced by half. Add the butter to enrich the gravy, swirling the pan around to emulsify.

Serve a good slice of suckling pig on each plate with some of the gravy poured over, garnished with watercress and pickled vegetables.

Vignole is a wonderful thing: a glorious green stew of artichokes, peas and broad beans enriched with lardo, it's perfect with slow-braised pork belly melting within it. At the restaurant, we cook the pork belly for 15 hours in a water bath, but the recipe below has been adapted for home cooking.

Slow-braised Pork Belly with Vignole

Serves: 4

Preparation time: 30 minutes

Cooking time: 2 hours

600g pork belly, cut into 4 equal slices, approximately 2.5cm thick

sea salt and freshly ground black pepper

olive oil

4 slices of lardo, 1–2mm thick

1 onion, thinly sliced

2 garlic cloves, crushed

1 sprig of fresh thyme

1 bay leaf

1 glass of white wine

500ml Chicken Stock (see page 216)

4 violet artichokes, left whole, stems trimmed to 3cm

1 handful of shelled peas, blanched and refreshed

1 handful of shelled broad beans, blanched and refreshed

80g butter

1 sprig of fresh mint, finely chopped

Season the slices of pork with salt and pepper, then heat some olive oil in an ovenproof casserole dish and seal them on both sides until golden. Remove and set aside.

Add the lardo, onion, garlic, thyme and bay leaf to the casserole and cook really slowly, with no colour. Add the wine and cook until reduced by half, then put the pork back and add the chicken stock. Cover with a lid and simmer for approximately 1 hour, or until tender.

Meanwhile, boil the artichokes for 10–12 minutes, or until tender, then drain and refresh in cold water. Drain again, then remove and discard the outer leaves and the furry choke and cut into quarters.

Remove the cooked pork from the casserole and set aside. Add the peas, broad beans and artichokes to the stock and season again if necessary. Bring to the boil, then lower the heat and simmer for 10 minutes. Add the butter and stir in to enrich the stock.

Add the mint, then return the pork to the casserole. Allow to sit for 5 minutes, then serve in bowls, finished with a drizzle of olive oil.

Serves: 4

Preparation time: 20 minutes

Cooking time: 2 hours

olive oil

2 onions, finely sliced

500ml Chicken Stock (see page 216), simmered until concentrated and reduced by half

2 tablespoons grain mustard

2 sprigs of fresh parsley, chopped

For the faggots

200g mutton shoulder, minced

100g mutton liver, minced

2 mutton kidneys, minced

200g streaky bacon, minced

100g breadcrumbs

1 onion, finely diced and cooked gently with no colour

½ teaspoon ground mace

½ teaspoon ground allspice

1 sprig of fresh rosemary, finely chopped

sea salt and freshly ground black pepper

caul fat, to wrap

For the beetroot and celeriac relish

olive oil

1 teaspoon yellow mustard seeds

1 teaspoon onion seeds

1 sprig of fresh rosemary

200g beetroots, roasted and finely chopped

200g celeriac, finely diced and blanched

1 onion, finely chopped

50g caster sugar

50ml water

50ml cider vinegar

seeds of 2 cardamom pods

Faggots are an old British classic that should be cooked more at home. We make them with mutton, to help with the mutton renaissance, but you can easily swap the meat for pork. Make sure you have lots of crusty bread to hand, or failing that a good scoop of mash.

Mutton Faggots with Beetroot and Celeriac Relish

First, make the faggots. Put all the faggot ingredients, except the caul, into a bowl, mix well and season with salt and pepper. Shape the mixture into golfball-size balls and wrap them in the caul, ensuring it goes all the way round. Put them on a plate and place in the fridge until you need them.

Next, make the relish. Heat a splash of olive oil in a medium saucepan, add the mustard seeds, onion seeds and rosemary, and cook gently with no colour for about 5 minutes. The seeds may pop, so have a lid handy. Add all the other relish ingredients and cook gently for approximately 30 minutes, or until it has reduced to a chutney-like consistency.

Heat a little olive oil in another medium saucepan, add the sliced onions and cook slowly until a deep golden colour. Add the faggots and gently seal, taking care not to burn the onions.

Now add the stock and gently simmer for 20 minutes. Add the mustard, give it a good stir and finish with the chopped parsley. Serve with plenty of relish and lots of crusty bread.

Serves: 4

Preparation time: 1 hour, plus chilling and cooling

Cooking time: 2 hours

For the ragout

olive oil

3 rabbit legs, on the bone

2 slices of pancetta, finely diced

2 shallots, finely diced

2 sticks of celery, finely diced

3 garlic cloves, finely diced

3 sprigs of fresh rosemary, leaves picked and finely chopped

3 sprigs of fresh sage, leaves picked and finely chopped

1 glass of white wine

2 litres Chicken Stock (see page 216)

sea salt and freshly grated black pepper

50g Parmesan cheese, grated

For the pasta

500g '00' pasta flour

5 large eggs

plain flour, for dusting

semolina, for dusting

To garnish

50g butter

8 fresh sage leaves

aged pecorino cheese, or Parmesan

You will also need a pasta machine

The River Café is one of my favourite restaurants. It's an example of what a restaurant should be, and indeed how food should be: the finest ingredients cooked with love, care and attention in a warm and friendly environment. Before we opened Duck & Waffle I spent a day in their kitchen, and this is a version of one of the dishes I learnt that day – I was drawn to the pasta station almost immediately...

Rabbit Agnoli with Sage Brown Butter

First, make the rabbit ragout. Heat a little olive oil in a medium saucepan, then add the rabbit legs and brown them on all sides. Take out and place on a plate, then add the pancetta, shallots, celery, garlic, rosemary and sage to the pan and cook gently for 8–10 minutes, but with no colour. Put the rabbit legs back into the pan, add the wine and simmer until reduced by half. Add enough chicken stock to cover, season with salt and pepper, then lower the heat and simmer slowly for about 1½ hours, or until the meat comes away from the bone easily.

Next, make the pasta. Put the flour and eggs into a mixing bowl and mix together really well, kneading until smooth. Cover the bowl with clingfilm and put in the fridge.

When the rabbit legs are ready, take them out of the pan and set aside. Discard all but 500ml of the stock and simmer it until reduced by three-quarters. When the rabbit is cool enough to handle, flake it into tiny pieces, or finely chop, and put back into the pan. Mix really well, and if there is any liquid remaining, cook until it has evaporated but not totally dried out. Allow to cool, then add the Parmesan and set aside.

Using a pasta machine, roll out your pasta gradually, starting from the thickest setting down to the thinnest. Fold the pasta back together and repeat. It should be super-stretchy. Lay out the pasta on a floured surface, and on one half of the sheet put grape-size balls of the rabbit mixture, allowing 4cm free all around. You should be able to make 24 agnoli (6 per person) from this amount of pasta. Run your finger, dipped in cold water, around the sides of the filling, then fold over the other half of the pasta and gently press down so it sticks, avoiding any air. Cut out rectangles, approximately 6 x 4cm, between the mounds of filling. Take diagonal opposite corners and pinch together, like a small parcel. Store in the fridge, on a baking sheet dusted with semolina.

When ready to cook, bring a large saucepan of salted water to the boil and cook your agnoli for 3 minutes.

Heat the butter and sage leaves in a separate saucepan and allow to foam. When the leaves are crisp, remove with a slotted spoon, drain on kitchen paper and reserve. Strain the pasta and add to the pan of foaming butter. Allow the butter to brown a little, then transfer the pasta to serving plates. Add a good grating of aged pecorino, a drizzle of the brown butter, the crispy sage leaves and a touch of olive oil to finish.

This is my favourite pasta dish from our restaurant menu and has been the most well-received, using the best of winter veg – Jerusalem artichokes. Making pasta is so rewarding and relaxing, and every time you make it you learn so much and can see yourself improving. Once you feel comfortable, experiments with various shapes will begin.

Jerusalem Artichoke and Truffle Ravioli

Serves: 6 (5 ravioli per person)
Preparation time: 1 ½ hours, plus chilling
Cooking time: 30 minutes

For the pasta
500g 'OO' pasta flour
5 large eggs
plain flour, for dusting
semolina, for dusting

For the filling
olive oil
500g Jerusalem artichokes, peeled and cut into 2.5cm pieces
200ml double cream
50g Parmesan cheese, finely grated
sea salt and freshly ground black pepper
20g truffle (fresh if possible, or slices in oil), finely chopped

To finish
60g butter
10 turnip leaves, finely chopped
50g hazelnuts, roasted and crushed
aged pecorino cheese, or Parmesan, grated just before cooking

You will also need a pasta machine

First, make the pasta. Put the flour and eggs into a bowl and mix together really well, kneading until smooth. Cover with clingfilm and put into the fridge for 30 minutes.

Now make the filling. Heat a little olive oil in a medium saucepan and cook the artichokes gently for 8 minutes. Add the cream and lower the heat. Let the artichokes simmer until soft, at which point use a slotted spoon to remove them from the cream, put them into a food processor and blitz until smooth. If the mixture is too thick, add a little of the cream from the pan. Allow the purée to cool, then add the Parmesan, salt, pepper and truffle.

Using a pasta machine, roll out your pasta gradually, starting from the thickest setting down to the thinnest it will go, about 0.5mm. Fold the pasta back together and repeat. It should be super-stretchy. Lay out the pasta on a floured surface, and on one half of the sheet put grape-size blobs of the artichoke purée, allowing 3cm free all around. You should be able to make 30 ravioli from this amount of pasta. Run your finger, dipped in cold water, around the sides of the filling, then fold over the other half of the pasta and gently press down so that it sticks, avoiding any air. Cut out the ravioli between the mounds of filling with a cookie cutter, one that allows a 2–3cm rim around the filling – a 6cm one should do. Store in the fridge, on a baking sheet dusted with semolina.

When ready to cook, bring a large saucepan of salted water to the boil and cook your ravioli for 3 minutes.

In another saucepan, melt the butter and gently cook the turnip leaves for 2 minutes, or until just wilted. Using a slotted spoon, remove the ravioli from the water and add to the butter and turnip leaves. Add a tablespoon of the pasta water and let it bubble so that the sauce emulsifies. Keep the pasta moving at all times to avoid them frying like dumplings.

Turn out on to a serving dish and garnish with the crushed hazelnuts and freshly grated pecorino (or Parmesan).

DESSERTS

Serves: 12

Preparation time: 2 days
(if making it all from scratch)

Cooking time: 30 minutes

1 (397ml) tin of condensed milk

1 handful of Honeycomb (see page 219), crushed into 1cm pieces

For the peanut butter ice cream

500ml milk

500ml double cream

1 vanilla pod

190g caster sugar

4 tablespoons smooth peanut butter

10 egg yolks

For the marshmallow

70g golden syrup

45g caster sugar

25ml water

1 egg white

a small pinch of salt

For the brownie

280g dark chocolate (70% cocoa)

280g unsalted butter

400g caster sugar

6 eggs

130g plain flour, sifted

60g cocoa powder, sifted

170g white chocolate chunks

You will also need a sugar thermometer

This is a dish, that in one form or another, has been on the restaurant menu since we opened. I know every chef and home cook alike states that they have the greatest brownie recipe ever, but, believe me, look no further, it's here... It has now evolved into a sundae, which you can do too by simply layering up the various elements in a tall glass. If you have any caramelized nuts lying around, they make a great addition – hazelnuts, almonds, peanuts, all work perfectly, as does a dollop of Chantilly cream on the top.

Brownies with Peanut Butter Ice Cream and Marshmallow

DAY 1

First, place the unopened tin of condensed milk in a saucepan and cover with water. Bring to the boil, then lower the heat and cook at a simmer for 4 hours, making sure you top up the water throughout so that the tin is always submerged. Allow to cool. When cool, open the tin – a caramel will have formed. Spoon out into a bowl, cover with clingfilm and leave in the fridge until ready to use.

To make the ice cream, bring the milk, cream and vanilla to the boil in a large saucepan. Meanwhile, put the sugar, peanut butter and egg yolks into a bowl and whisk very well. (Sugar absorbs moisture, and if you don't mix straight away you will have pieces of dried egg yolk where all the moisture has been removed by the sugar, so beware.)

Once the milk and cream comes to the boil, pour half on to the yolk mix and whisk together. Pour this back into the remaining milk and cream in the saucepan and heat gently until thickened. In the kitchen we use a thermometer to check once it is cooked – 84°C is the temperature we take it to (any higher and the egg will scramble, leaving your ice cream lumpy) – but if you don't have one, cook until the mixture coats the back of a wooden spoon and stays there without running off straight away. Strain the mixture, transfer to another bowl to stop it cooking, then cool and churn.

If you don't have an ice cream machine, freeze the mixture in four batches and, once frozen, blend in a food processor. Return to the freezer after blending.

If you don't have honeycomb to hand, now's the time to make it (see page 219).

To make the marshmallow, place the golden syrup, sugar and water in a saucepan and, over a medium heat, cook to 117°C on a sugar thermometer. In the meantime, whisk the egg white and salt together until fluffy. Slowly add the syrup mix, the same as when making Italian meringue (see page 160), and continue whisking until the mixture is thick and the bowl has cooled. Spoon out into a container and store in the fridge.

Continued over the page

DAY 2

Now make your brownie. Preheat your oven to 180°C/gas mark 4, and line a 35 x 25cm baking tin with baking paper.

Put the chocolate and butter into a heatproof bowl and set it over a saucepan of gently simmering water until melted. In a mixing bowl, whisk the sugar and eggs together until light and fluffy. Add the chocolate mix to the egg mix and fold in, then fold in the sifted flour and cocoa powder. Fold in the white chocolate and put the mixture into the prepared baking tin. Place in the oven and bake for 20 minutes. It may look undercooked when you take it out, but when it's cooled it will be perfect and soft.

To serve, there are no real rules. At the restaurant, we spread the marshmallow over the bottom of the plate and blowtorch it to give it a nice toasty taste. Then we simply cut the brownie into squares (doesn't have to be perfect), and serve with a good scoop of ice cream, some crumbled honeycomb and a spoonful of the dulce de leche caramel.

This is what Tom does when he's hungry and hung over; he makes kickass desserts. It started off as a cure, then became one of our best-selling dessert specials to date. If it's on the board, you know someone's feeling tender.

Cherry Cola Float

Makes: 2

Preparation time: 10 minutes

Cooking time: none

2 scoops of Vanilla Ice Cream (see page 219)

100g cherries, stoned

½ a can of cola

25ml grenadine

Put a scoop of ice cream into the bottom of each sundae glass, or use bowls if you don't have those.

Divide the cherries between the glasses, then pour over the cola, a quarter of a can per glass. Drizzle with the grenadine to finish.

This is one of my all-time favourite desserts. It requires a bit of preparation, but once the elements are done, it's relatively straightforward to make and have ready in the freezer for whenever you need to wow your friends. The toasty meringue reminds me of marshmallows charred on the fire, and the cold ice cream complements it perfectly.

Baked Alaska with Strawberry Juice

Serves: 6

Preparation time: 1 hour, plus cooling, chilling and freezing

Cooking time: 1 hour

6 balls of Vanilla Ice Cream (see page 219), frozen hard

For the dulce de leche sponge

75g unsalted butter, at room temperature, plus extra for greasing

30g golden syrup

1 (397ml) tin of dulce de leche (milk caramel)

2 eggs

100g self-raising flour

For the strawberry juice

300g strawberries

75ml strawberry liqueur (you can substitute another fruity liqueur, or rum)

15g caster sugar

For the Italian meringue

225g caster sugar

150ml water

90g egg whites

You will also need a sugar thermometer and a piping bag with a plain 10mm nozzle

Preheat the oven to 180°C/gas mark 4. Lightly grease a 30cm lipped baking tray and cover with baking paper.

To make the sponge, put the softened butter, golden syrup and dulce de leche (milk caramel) into a mixing bowl and, using an electric mixer, or a wooden spoon if doing by hand, cream together until lighter in colour – this should take about 5 minutes. Crack the eggs into a bowl and whisk together. Still creaming the butter mix, add the eggs, then mix together for another 2 minutes, or until completely smooth. Sift in the flour and mix for 1 more minute. Spoon your sponge mix on to the prepared baking tray and spread out until it is 1cm thick. Bake in the oven for 8–10 minutes, then remove and cool on a wire rack. Using a 10cm diameter cookie cutter, cut out 6 discs of sponge and set aside.

To make the strawberry juice, wash the strawberries, take the green tops off with a small knife, and cut them in half or quarters if large. Place in a metal bowl, add the liqueur and sugar, cover tightly with clingfilm and place over a saucepan of simmering water, making sure the bottom of the bowl doesn't touch the water. Leave to simmer for 30 minutes, then turn off the heat. Once cooled a little, strain off and discard the pulp. Place the liquid in the fridge to chill.

To make the meringue, put the sugar into a small saucepan over a low heat and gently pour over the water. Make sure no sugar has come up the sides of the pan, as this will make the syrup crystallize. Put the egg whites into a mixing bowl and, using an electric hand mixer, whisk on slow speed. Once the sugar has reached 116°C, increase the speed of whisking to create soft peaks. When the sugar has reached 121°C, pour it slowly on to the egg whites while still whisking on a high speed. Once the sugar syrup has been added, continue to whisk until the meringue has cooled to room temperature, then put into a piping bag with a plain 10mm nozzle.

To finish, put the sponge discs on individual pieces of baking paper on a baking sheet and place a ball of ice cream on each sponge disc. Pipe the meringue all the way around, to completely cover. At this stage place in the freezer until you are ready to cook and serve.

When ready to cook, preheat your oven to 200°C/gas mark 6. Place the baking sheet on the bottom shelf for 3 minutes, or until the meringue is nice and browned. Carefully transfer to serving bowls and pour the strawberry juice around.

If a Sunday roast were part of my last meal on this planet, then a steamed pudding would have to be the dessert. The classic treacle sponge with custard is divine, but at the restaurant we add some wintry orange notes to the dish. Restaurants in England often offer custard or ice cream with puddings; try both, I certainly wouldn't blame you if you did. It's exactly what I do.

Steamed Orange Puddings with Grand Marnier Custard

Serves: 6

Preparation time: 30 minutes

Cooking time: 1 hour 20 minutes

190g unsalted butter, softened, plus extra for greasing

190g caster sugar

2 oranges

3 eggs

130g plain flour

15g baking powder

100g breadcrumbs

For the orange syrup

160g caster sugar

1 litre orange juice

For the Grand Marnier custard

225ml milk

225ml double cream

3 egg yolks

45g caster sugar

30ml Grand Marnier

Grease six 160ml dariole moulds with butter and set aside.

To make the puddings, cream the butter and sugar in a mixer until light in colour. Meanwhile, zest both oranges but only juice 1 of them. Add the juice and zest to the bowl once the butter and sugar have creamed, then mix again and add the eggs. Continue to mix, making sure to scrape down the sides. The mixture will split, but don't worry, it will come back together. Now add the flour, baking powder and breadcrumbs and make sure it's really well mixed.

Spoon the mixture into the moulds, filling them two-thirds full, leaving 1cm free at the top. Cover with foil and use elastic bands or string to hold the foil in place.

Place in a steamer over a medium heat, so that there is lots of steam, for 40 minutes.

While the puddings are cooking, make the syrup and custard.

To make the syrup, put the sugar and orange juice into a saucepan and bring to the boil. Continually skimming off any foam, cook until it has reduced to about 200ml.

To make the custard, heat the milk and cream in a saucepan. Meanwhile, put the egg yolks, sugar and Grand Marnier into a bowl and whisk together. Once the milk and cream mixture has boiled, slowly pour it on to the yolk mix and stir well. Put the mixture into a clean saucepan and heat gently until it thickens a little, taking care not scramble the eggs and make it go lumpy. Pass through a sieve and set aside until the sponge is ready.

To serve, spoon some of the custard into each bowl and add the puddings fresh from the steamer. Finish by spooning over the syrup, about 2 tablespoons per pud.

I love the freshness of this dish, but it is dependent on the quality of the fruit. As the ice cream sits on the hot peaches and runs into the honey, it looks so tempting. Italian fruit, in the peak of the season, is hard to beat. As the seasons change, try the same dish with ripe British pears – plums work great too.

Roasted Peaches with Thyme, Honey and Saffron Sponge

Serves: 4

Preparation time: 30 minutes

Cooking time: 50 minutes

4 ripe peaches, halved and stones removed

8 small sprigs of fresh thyme

6 tablespoons runny honey

4 scoops of Vanilla Ice Cream (see page 219)

For the saffron sponge

50g unsalted butter, melted, plus extra for greasing

4 eggs

125g caster sugar

a pinch of saffron

125g plain flour

To make the sponge, preheat your oven to 180°C/gas mark 4. Grease a 28 x 22cm rectangular cake tin and line it with baking paper.

Put the eggs, sugar and saffron into a bowl and whisk over a saucepan of gently simmering water until light and fluffy. Take off the heat and gently fold in the flour, then add the melted butter. Pour into the prepared tin, and bake for approximately 15–20 minutes, or until a skewer comes out clean when inserted into the centre. When baking, try not to open the door until 15 minutes has passed so as not to disturb the rising. Turn out on to a wire rack and leave to cool.

Place the peaches, cut side up, in a roasting tin lined with baking paper. Place a sprig of thyme on top of each peach half and drizzle over the honey. Roast in the oven for approximately 15 minutes, basting the peaches with the honey every 3–4 minutes.

To serve, tear the sponge into 4 small biscuit-size pieces per person, and add 2 halves of peach per plate. Add a scoop of ice cream and a good drizzle of the thyme honey, using some leaves too – it's all added flavour.

These are ideal little nibbles to have up your sleeve, whether to indulge a sudden sweet craving or to whip out at the end of a meal. Beats buying chocolates – you'll have worked for your reward!

Homemade Chocolates and Nibbles

Makes: 50 x 2.5cm pieces
Preparation time: 10 minutes
Cooking time: 15 minutes

15g gelatine leaves

oil, for greasing

cornflour or icing sugar, for dusting

100ml water

200g sugar

40g liquid glucose

80g egg whites

120g lemon curd

30g ready-made meringue nests, broken into small pieces

50g icing sugar

50g cornflour

You will also need a sugar thermometer

LEMON MARSHMALLOWS

Put the gelatine leaves into very cold water to soak and become soft.
Grease a 20cm springform cake tin and dust it lightly with cornflour or icing sugar.

Carefully put the water, sugar and glucose into a saucepan, making sure the sugar does not go up the sides. Bring to the boil and put in a sugar thermometer. Once it reaches 116°C, put the egg whites into a mixing bowl and, using an electric hand mixer, start whisking. When the sugar reaches 121°C, turn off the heat and finish whisking the whites until stiff peaks form.

Now slowly pour the sugar syrup into the whites, whisking all the time. Drain the gelatine leaves and add them to the mixture while it is still hot. Whisk for 2 minutes, then add the lemon curd and meringue and continue to whisk.

When the mixture is cold, stop whisking and pour it into the prepared cake tin. Level the top with a wet palette knife, and put into the fridge for 1 hour to set. Remove and cut to the desired shape.

Sift the icing sugar and cornflour together and roll your marshmallows in this until they are well coated (this is to stop the marshmallows sticking together). Now they are ready to serve.

Makes: 200g
Preparation time: 5 minutes
Cooking time: 20 minutes

200g almonds, shelled and skinned

60g caster sugar

50ml water

100g cocoa powder

You will also need a sugar thermometer

COCOA ALMONDS

Preheat your oven to 160°C/gas mark 3. Place the almonds on a baking sheet and roast in the oven for 8–10 minutes, or until golden brown.

Put the sugar and water into a saucepan and bring to the boil. Put in a sugar thermometer and heat until the sugar has reached 116°C. As there is quite a small amount of syrup, you may have to tip the pan to be able to get a reading on your thermometer, so do be careful not to burn yourself.

Add the hot nuts and stir vigorously – eventually the sugar will crystallize and leave a fine coating around each nut. Return the pan to a low heat and continue to cook until the sugar caramelizes. Once each nut is golden brown, take off the heat and add the cocoa powder. Stir until well coated, then put into a sieve to get rid of any excess cocoa. Turn out on to a baking sheet lined with baking paper and leave to cool.

Makes: 50

Preparation time: 30 minutes, plus cooling, chilling and freezing

Cooking time: 4¼ hours

1 (397ml) tin of condensed milk

a pinch of sea salt

200g dark chocolate (70% cocoa solids), broken into pieces

SALTED CARAMEL TRUFFLES

Beware – this is a bit of a messy recipe, so don't be scared of getting your hands dirty!

First, place the unopened tin of condensed milk in a large saucepan and cover with water. Bring to the boil, then lower the heat and simmer for 4 hours, making sure you top up the water throughout so the tin is always submerged. Take out and allow to cool for 30 minutes.

When cool, open the tin and spoon out the caramel into a bowl, add the salt and mix well. Chill in the fridge for 30 minutes so it firms up a bit – you'll find it much easier to work with.

Once chilled, use a teaspoon to make balls the size of a small marble and place on a plate. Put into the freezer for 2 hours, or until firm.

Melt the chocolate in a heatproof bowl set over a saucepan of gently simmering water. Line a baking sheet with baking paper. Put on plastic gloves (so as not to make too much mess), and take the balls out of the freezer. Coat your gloves with melted chocolate, roll one ball and place on the prepared baking sheet. Repeat the process until all the balls are coated. Put into the fridge for about 1 hour to set the chocolate and to allow the caramel to defrost and soften.

Makes: 8

Preparation time: 1 hour

Cooking time: 1 hour

For the peanut brittle

200g unsalted peanuts

60g caster sugar

a small pinch of sea salt

For the Italian meringue

150g caster sugar

100ml water

60g egg whites

For the macaroons

150g ground almonds

150g icing sugar

a pinch of red food colouring powder, or a few drops of liquid colouring

60g egg whites

For the peanut butter mousse

200g Crème Pâtissière (see page 19)

2 tablespoons smooth peanut butter

2 tablespoons cream cheese

100ml double cream, whipped to soft peaks

To assemble

4 tablespoons raspberry jam

2 bananas

caster sugar, for sprinkling

2 punnets of raspberries

You will also need a sugar thermometer and a piping bag fitted with a plain nozzle

PBJ – peanut butter and jam – is such a classic. What I love most is how it can be interpreted in so many ways. We make it classically as a toasted sandwich for brunch, then offer a more refined dessert option for dinner. Every time I eat this my brain is thinking of other ways to use it, maybe a PBJ doughnut, cheesecake or sundae…

PBJ Macaroon

To make the brittle, preheat the oven to 160°C/gas mark 3. Roast the peanuts for approximately 10 minutes. Once they are roasted, put the sugar and salt into a saucepan and put over a low heat. Allow to caramelize until dark golden – this will give a better flavour, but don't let it get too dark or it will taste bitter. Add the hot nuts and stir quickly, then, using a metal spoon, place on a sheet of baking paper and allow to cool. Once cold, you can blitz the brittle in a food processor or chop it by hand.

Preheat your oven to 160°C/gas mark 3 again.

To make the meringue, put the sugar into a saucepan and gently pour over the water. Make sure no sugar comes up the sides of the pan, as this will make the syrup crystallize.

Put the egg whites into a mixing bowl and whisk on slow speed. Once the sugar has reached 116°C on a sugar thermometer, increase the speed of whisking to create soft peaks. When the sugar has reached 121°C, pour it slowly on to the whites while still whisking on a high speed. Once the sugar syrup has been added, continue to whisk until it has cooled down to room temperature.

Sift the ground almonds and icing sugar into a bowl and add the food colouring. Add the egg whites and make a paste, using a wooden spoon or scraper. Now beat in the Italian meringue, using a mixer or by hand, until it becomes runnier. To check when it is ready to pipe, spoon a small amount on to a plate and if the peak disappears in 1 minute it is ready.

With a pencil, draw circles with a 10cm diameter on a sheet of baking paper, then turn over so the pencilled side is underneath and place on a baking sheet. Following the lines you can see through the paper, pipe the mixture in a spiral to fill the space.

Place in the oven for 20 minutes, then remove and allow to cool.

To make the mousse, whisk the crème pâtissière and peanut butter together, then add the cream cheese and mix well. Fold in the whipped cream and place in a piping bag.

To assemble, put ½ tablespoon of jam on each macaroon and spread it out.

Cut the banana into 5mm slices and sprinkle with caster sugar. Caramelize using a blowtorch if you have one, or put on a baking tray and caramelize under the grill. Place about 8 raspberries around the outside of each macaroon, and put 3 slices of caramelized banana in the centre. Carefully pipe the mousse over, creating a nice peak, like soft-serve ice cream.

Decorate with one further slice of caramelized banana, and sprinkle the peanut brittle over the top.

Makes: 4
Preparation time: 30 minutes
Cooking time: 25 minutes

oil, for deep-frying

1 bottle of ice-cold beer

200g plain flour,
plus extra for dusting

4 chocolate bars
(I use Mars™ bars)

For the malt ice cream

500ml double cream

500ml milk

4 tablespoons malt extract

seeds from 1 vanilla pod

190g caster sugar

10 egg yolks

For the oat crunch

150g plain flour

150g rolled oats
(porridge oats are fine)

150g unsalted butter

25g caster sugar

30ml milk

30g honey

You will also need a deep-fat fryer

We gave this a go on Burns Night and it went crazy. Naturally it went on the menu, but after a few weeks we had to take it off again. Sounds strange, but we couldn't keep up with the volume: when you have 5 or 6 in the fryer, the temperature drops, as does the standard of the batter. This makes far more oat crunch than you need, so you can either halve the quantities, freeze the dough in sausage-like tubes for later use, or have them with cheese – they're great as an alternative to crackers.

Deep-fried Chocolate Bar with Malt Ice Cream and Oat Crunch

To make the ice cream, bring the cream, milk, malt extract and vanilla to the boil in a large saucepan. Meanwhile, put the sugar and egg yolks in a bowl and whisk very well. (Sugar absorbs moisture, and if you don't mix straight away you will have pieces of dried egg yolk where all the moisture has been removed by the sugar, so beware.)

Once the milk and cream comes to the boil, pour half on to the yolk mix and whisk together. Pour this back into the remaining milk and cream in the pan and heat gently until thickened. In the kitchen we use a thermometer to check when it's ready – 84°C is the temperature we take it to (any higher and the egg will scramble, leaving your ice cream lumpy) – but if you don't have one, cook until the mixture coats the back of a wooden spoon and stays there without running off straight away. Strain the mixture, transfer to another bowl to stop it cooking, then cool and churn in an ice cream machine. If you don't have an ice cream machine, freeze the mix in four batches and, once frozen, blend in a food processor. Return to the freezer after blending. (Alternatively, you could make a plain vanilla base (see page 219) and just before churning add the malt extract – this saves you making multiple ice creams. If you already have plain vanilla ice cream, you can drizzle the extract over to get the flavour too.)

To make the oat crunch, put the flour, oats, butter and sugar into a mixing bowl and mix in a food mixer with a paddle attachment on low speed, or with an electric hand mixer. Put the milk and honey into a small saucepan and heat gently until the honey melts and it becomes one liquid. Once the butter has been rubbed into the flour, oats and sugar, pour in the milk and honey. As soon as it has combined, stop mixing. Make the mixture into two long sausage shapes, then wrap them in clingfilm and roll them so they become tight. Chill them in the fridge for 2 hours – they are then ready to cut and cook.

Preheat your oven to 180°C/gas mark 4 and line a baking sheet with baking paper. Unwrap the oat sausages and use a sharp knife to cut them into slices about 7mm thick (a little either way won't matter too much). Place them evenly on the prepared baking sheet and bake for 7–10 minutes, or until they have a nice golden colour. Set aside to cool. (These can be made ahead of time and stored in an airtight container.)

When ready to serve, heat the oil to 180°C in your deep-fat fryer.

Slowly whisk the beer into the flour to make a smooth batter with the consistency of thick custard. Remove the wrappers from the chocolate bars, and dust each one with flour. Coat with the batter and carefully drop into the fryer. Cook for about 3 minutes, or until the batter is crispy.

Drain on kitchen paper, and serve in a bowl with a good scoop of malt ice cream and a couple of oat crunch biscuits crumbled over.

Cheese and port is a very popular combination, so working on the idea of deep red fruit flavours and cheese, we adapted the Lancashire classic by adding a knob of blue cheese inside. As the cakes bake the cheese bubbles away and comes through the slices in the pastry, so that they become beautifully rustic. Try these instead of a cheese board at the end of a meal. Stilton is fine to substitute if you can't get hold of Fourme d'Ambert.

Fourme d'Ambert Eccles Cakes

Makes: 12

Preparation time: 20 minutes, plus chilling

Cooking time: 20 minutes

30g unsalted butter, melted

150g soft brown sugar

120g currants

½ teaspoon freshly grated nutmeg

¼ teaspoon ground allspice

¼ teaspoon ground cinnamon

finely grated zest and juice of ¼ of an orange

500g puff pastry, rolled out into sheets 5mm thick

300g Fourme d'Ambert cheese, cut into 12 x 2cm cubes

milk, for glazing

caster sugar, for dusting

Put the butter, sugar, currants, spices, orange zest and juice into a bowl and mix well. Take a teaspoon of the mixture and roll it into a ball. Continue until you have 12 balls.

Take the pastry sheets and, using a cookie cutter, cut out discs approximately 10cm in diameter. Place a cube of cheese in the centre of each pastry, then top with one of the fruit mix balls, flattened slightly. Brush the sides of the pastry with milk, then turn them up to enclose the mix and seal. Turn them over and place on a baking sheet lined with baking paper. Place in the fridge to rest for 30 minutes.

Preheat your oven to 180°C/gas mark 4. Take the cakes from the fridge, make 3 slashes on the top and brush with milk. Dust with sugar and bake for approximately 20 minutes, or until golden brown.

Pistachio and rose is such a wonderful combination and one that you'll find in many cuisines, including Turkish and Indian, to name but a few. The deep, fresh nutty flavour is subtly complemented by the floral rose – add sweetened cream and fresh summer raspberries and the balance is just perfect. This can be a tray bake-style cake to take to work, or a glorious masterpiece with swirls of cream, that becomes a beautiful mess once broken into.

Pistachio and Olive Oil Cake with Rose-scented Chantilly Cream

Serves: 8–12
Preparation time: 30 minutes
Cooking time: 45–55 minutes

For the cake

100g unsalted butter, plus extra for greasing

200g green pistachios

50g polenta

50g plain flour

5g baking powder

grated zest and juice of ½ a lemon

grated zest and juice of ½ an orange

125ml olive oil

3 eggs

200g caster sugar

For the rose-scented Chantilly cream

225ml double cream

30g caster sugar

¼ teaspoon rose water or rose essence

To decorate

fresh raspberries, about 6 per person

50g icing sugar, for dusting

Preheat your oven to 160°C/gas mark 3. Lightly grease a 23cm springform cake tin.

Put the nuts into a food processor and begin to blend them. When they are nearly all blended, stop the machine, add the polenta, flour and baking powder, then continue blending until they have a coarsely ground texture. Transfer them to a bowl and add the orange and lemon zest and juice.

Gently warm the butter in a small saucepan. Once melted, add the oil and set aside.

Crack the eggs into a mixing bowl, add the sugar and whisk for 5 minutes (the mixture should double in size, if not more). Add the butter and oil mixture, and once all is combined stop the machine and fold in your pistachio mix. Pour the mixture into the prepared cake tin and bake for approximately 45 minutes. (It should be nice and golden on top and a skewer, when inserted, should come out clean.) Allow to cool on a wire rack.

To prepare the Chantilly cream, put the cream and sugar into a bowl. The strength of the rose water or essence that you find will change the recipe dramatically, so it's best to add it by taste, a little at a time – when you have enough rose flavour, stop and whisk all the ingredients together until stiff. Keep in the fridge until ready to serve.

Transfer the cake to a serving plate, spoon the Chantilly cream on top and decorate with the raspberries. Dust with icing sugar and serve immediately.

This is such a simple dessert, but we have pimped it with bacon. I've no idea why it works, but it just does. Don't be put off by the bacon – the smoky, salty edge that it gives really complements the rich sweet pudding. Give it a go...

Chocolate Bread Pudding with Bacon Custard

Serves: 8–10
Preparation time: 30 minutes
Cooking time: 1½ hours

For the pudding

150g unsalted butter, plus a little extra for greasing

140ml double cream

800ml milk

40g milk chocolate, roughly chopped

40g dark chocolate (70% cocoa), roughly chopped

4 egg yolks

140g caster sugar, plus extra for dusting

1 loaf of good-quality white bread, sliced and buttered

For the custard

6 rashers of smoked streaky bacon

150ml milk

150ml double cream

2 egg yolks

35g caster sugar

Preheat your oven to 140°C/gas mark 1 and butter an ovenproof dish approximately 28 x 23cm.

To make the pudding, put the cream and milk into a saucepan and bring to the boil, then add the chocolate and whisk in until melted. Remove from the heat. Whisk together the yolks and sugar in a bowl, then pour in the chocolate cream. Whisk well, then strain.

Use the butter to butter the bread, then layer it in the dish, with ladles of the chocolate custard in between. Press down with your fingers to make sure it is all soaked properly. Dust the top with a few pinches of sugar, and place in the oven for 30 minutes.

In the meantime, make your custard. Put the bacon into a medium saucepan and caramelize over a medium heat, pouring away any fat that comes out. When it's all brown, add the milk and cream and bring to the boil. Lower the heat and allow to infuse over a low heat for 30 minutes.

In a bowl, whisk together the egg yolks and sugar. Bring the cream back to the boil, and strain. Slowly pour the cream on to the yolk mix and stir well. Pour back into the pan and heat gently until it thickens a little – taking care not to let it scramble and go lumpy.

Serve the pudding with the custard poured over and around.

What every kid wants, and always a winner. The ice cream reminds me of Mini Milks and takes me straight back to my childhood. As for the freshly baked cookies, who doesn't love them? You can swap the dark chocolate for milk or white, and adding nuts is a great idea too.

Cookies and Milk

Serves: 8

Preparation time: 10 minutes, plus freezing

Cooking time: 30 minutes

For the milk ice cream

200ml double cream

800ml milk

200g caster sugar

8 egg yolks

For the cookies

115g unsalted butter

150g caster sugar

1 egg

170g dark chocolate chips

155g plain flour

¼ teaspoon baking powder

To make the milk ice cream, put the cream into a saucepan with 600ml of the milk and heat to just before boiling. While this is heating, put the sugar and egg yolks into a bowl and whisk very well. (Sugar absorbs moisture, and if you don't mix straight away you will have pieces of dried egg yolk where all the moisture has been removed by the sugar, so beware.)

Once the milk and cream comes to the boil, pour half on to the yolk mix and whisk together. Pour this back into the remaining milk and cream in the saucepan and heat gently until thickened. In the kitchen we use a thermometer to check when it's ready – 84°C is the temperature we take it to (any higher and the egg will scramble, leaving your ice cream lumpy) – but if you don't have one, cook until the mixture coats the back of a wooden spoon and stays there without running off straight away. Strain the mixture, transfer to another bowl to stop it cooking, then add the remaining 200ml of milk. It's done this way to maintain a fresh milk flavour. Allow to cool, then churn.

If you don't have an ice cream machine, freeze the mixture in four batches and, once frozen, blend in a food processor. Return to the freezer after blending.

Next, make the cookies. Preheat your oven to 160°C/gas mark 3. Line 2 baking sheets with baking paper.

Cream the butter and sugar together in a bowl, then add the egg, chocolate chips, flour and baking powder. Mix together until smooth, then roll into golfball-size balls – you should get 16 (2 per person). Place on the prepared baking sheets leaving room for them to expand, and flatten each one so they are 1cm thick. Bake for approximately 12–15 minutes, then cool on a rack.

Serve the ice cream in a bowl, with the freshly baked cookies on the side.

Jacek is always making little nibbles to get us through the long days and nights, and this is one of the best yet. It's so easy to make. I would keep this in mind if you find yourself making the peanut brittle or strawberry juice recipes and have a little left over – vanilla ice cream is generally to hand.

Praline-rolled Ice Cream with Strawberry Juice

Makes: 4

Preparation time: 10 minutes
(if not using leftovers, 30 minutes plus freezing)

Cooking time: none
(if not using leftovers, 30 minutes)

6 balls of Vanilla Ice Cream
(see page 219)

Peanut Brittle
(see page 168)

500ml Strawberry Juice
(see page 160)

This will be the shortest method in history. Take a ball of vanilla ice cream, roll it in peanut brittle until completely coated, and place in an espresso cup.

Add 3 tablespoons of strawberry juice, *et voilà*.

Rhubarb and custard, a childhood sweet-shop classic. Here we take the elements and build them up into a knickerbocker-glory style dessert, which looks and tastes amazing. This is one of my mum's favourites, so it had to go into the book. We make the shortbread into perfect round shapes, so any not used in this recipe look nice in your biscuit tin.

'Rhubarb and Custard'

Makes: 4

Preparation time: 1 hour

Cooking time: 1 hour 15 minutes

400g Crème Pâtissière (see page 19)

2kg rhubarb, peeled and sliced into 1cm pieces

170g caster sugar

1 star anise

50ml strawberry liqueur

200ml double cream

For the stock syrup

500g caster sugar

500ml water

juice of ½ a lemon

For the crème fraîche ice cream

500g crème fraîche

30ml lemon juice

For the shortbread

125g unsalted butter

55g caster sugar, plus extra for sprinkling

180g plain flour

First make the stock syrup. Combine all the ingredients together in a small saucepan and heat until the sugar has dissolved, then allow to cool.

To make the ice cream, combine the crème fraîche, lemon juice and 360ml stock syrup in a mixing bowl and whisk together until well blended. Place in an ice cream machine and churn until frozen. If you don't have an ice cream machine, freeze the mix in a couple of smaller batches, then, when frozen, blend in a food processor and return to the freezer immediately.

If you don't have the crème pâtissière made, now is the time to make it. Follow the steps on page 19.

Next, place the rhubarb in a saucepan with 150g of the sugar, the star anise and liqueur, and enough water to just cover. Bring to the boil, then lower the heat and simmer for 10 minutes. Strain and allow to cool. Save the strained syrup and simmer slowly to reduce to a honey-like consistency, then allow to cool; this will be used to decorate.

To make the shortbread, preheat your oven to 160°C/gas mark 3 and line a baking sheet with baking paper.

Mix the shortbread ingredients together with your fingers until well combined.

Roll out the mixture to 5mm thick, then, using a 10cm cookie cutter, cut out discs and place them on the prepared baking sheet. Keep mixing the trimmings together and re-rolling – there should be zero waste. Place in the fridge to firm up (about 30 minutes), then place in the oven for approximately 8 minutes, or until golden brown.

Dust with caster sugar as soon as they come out, and allow to cool.

Whip the cream and the remaining 20g of sugar to soft peaks, then fold it through the crème pâtissière.

To serve, build up layers of the custard, compote and slightly crumbled shortbread in a glass, like a sundae, and finish with a good scoop of crème fraîche ice cream and a drizzle of the rhubarb syrup.

SNACKS AND COCKTAILS

Arancini are probably the perfect snack – with so many variations, I never get bored with them. Originally created as a way to use up leftover risotto in Sicily, the rice is wrapped around a piece of mozzarella, breadcrumbed and deep-fried. The only challenge I have at home is making sure there is any risotto left! A lot of recipes will call for wine to be added before the stock, and I am one of the few that dislike this, but feel free to add a glass if you like – just make sure you reduce it until almost dry.

Arancini

Serves: 4 as a starter

Preparation time: 30 minutes, plus cooling

Cooking time: 1 hour

50ml olive oil

1 onion, finely chopped

1 garlic clove, finely chopped

1 sprig of fresh thyme

1 bay leaf

sea salt and freshly ground black pepper

150g Arborio risotto rice

500ml hot Chicken Stock (see page 216)

125g shelled fresh peas, or 125g frozen peas, defrosted

25g unsalted butter

¼ of a bunch of fresh mint, finely chopped

50g Parmesan cheese, grated

1 ball of mozzarella cheese, cut into 1cm cubes

100g plain flour

2 eggs, lightly beaten

100g breadcrumbs

vegetable oil, for frying

Heat the olive oil in a frying pan, add the onion, garlic, thyme and bay leaf and cook gently until soft, with no colour. Season with salt and pepper. Add the rice and give a good stir so that it gets slightly sealed by the heat, again with no colour.

Slowly start adding the hot stock, to just cover, and cook over a medium heat. When it starts to get dry, add more stock and continue in this way until the rice feels cooked. This should take around 20 minutes.

Stir in the peas, then add the butter, mint and Parmesan and fold in. Remove the thyme and bay leaf and season to taste. Place on a tray to cool, spreading it out as thinly as possible so it cools quicker.

When the rice has cooled, take a small amount, about half the size of a golfball, wrap it around a cube of mozzarella and roll it into a tight ball. Repeat with the rest of the rice and mozzarella. Roll the balls in flour, shake off the excess, then dip in the beaten eggs, and finally finish by rolling in the breadcrumbs.

At this stage you can refrigerate the arancini for later use – put them into airtight containers, layered on baking paper, and they will keep in the fridge for up to 2 days. If you are going to cook them straight away, heat the oil to 180°C in your deep-fat fryer or in a deep heavy-based saucepan and fry them gently for 3–4 minutes. Drain on kitchen paper, and season lightly with salt.

VARIATIONS

There are so many possibilities here, the list is endless. Two of my favourites are Pumpkin and Ricotta, and Tomato, Basil and Mozzarella. Give them a go – they're always a winner.

We spent a good few months working on the recipe for our house bread. A big shout out here to chefs Emilio Solano and Chris Thompson for this development. Emilio took the bread to one level, and then Chris took it to where it is today. When you have perfectionists working with a product day in, day out, they get pretty damn good at it. At the restaurant we have a brick oven, so we cook the dough directly on the brick base at a very high temperature, this way the bread cooks super-quick. At home, you can either use a griddle and cook directly on it, or you can bake the bread in a regular oven. For the plain house bread I'd recommend the griddle, as essentially it's a variation of a naan dough, and griddling really lends itself to this style of bread. For the recipes with toppings, the oven will work best.

House Breads

Makes: 6

Preparation time: 20 minutes, plus proving time (approximately 2 hours)

Cooking time: 15 minutes

240ml water, at room temperature

8g fresh yeast

80g natural yoghurt

400g plain flour

6g baking powder

6g sea salt

olive oil, for greasing

Combine the water, yeast and yoghurt in a bowl and leave at room temperature for 10 minutes. In another bowl, combine the flour, baking powder and salt.

Add the water mix to the flour mix and ensure all is incorporated evenly. Continue to knead for 5 minutes in the bowl. Don't be scared if the dough is wet, that's the way it should be. Cover with a wet cloth and allow to prove for approximately 2 hours.

When the dough has proved, knock any air out and divide into 100–120g balls. You may find that because the dough is quite wet, it's hard to manipulate. Feel free to add a little extra flour to your hands to help. Place the balls of dough on oiled baking sheets and cover with a tea towel. If not using straight away, place in the fridge at this point.

Preheat your oven to 200°C/gas mark 6, or heat a griddle pan over a medium heat.

When ready to use, take the dough balls out of the fridge and leave on the side for about 10–15 minutes so that they rise again. Pat them down slightly to form a flat surface (about 15cm in diameter), then either place in the oven for 12–15 minutes or, if using a griddle, oil lightly and griddle for 2–3 minutes on each side.

VARIATIONS

Before baking, after you have flattened the dough balls, add whichever combination of topping ingredients you choose – here are some of my favourites:

goat's cheese and wild mushrooms (opposite, above)

confit garlic and rosemary (opposite, below)

caramelized onions, brown anchovy fillets and capers

n'duja and Gruyère

Having the luxury of a brick oven at the restaurant meant the chefs would inevitably start making themselves pizzas as a snack. Below is our pizza dough recipe, which was created by our Italians (at one point, around January 2013, we had nine Italians in the kitchen, so you can only imagine). The various flavour variations below are a reflection of how chefs eat at various times of the day.

Pizzette

Makes: 6
Preparation time: 1½ hours
Cooking time: 10–12 minutes

For the dough

400g strong white flour, plus extra for dusting

125g semolina flour

2 teaspoons sea salt

12g fresh yeast / 1 sachet of fast-acting instant yeast

300ml lukewarm water

50ml olive oil

For the topping

3 tablespoons olive oil, plus extra for greasing

2 onions, finely chopped

4 garlic cloves, finely chopped

2 small dried chillies (optional)

sea salt and freshly ground black pepper

2 (400g) tins of plum tomatoes

1 bunch of fresh basil, roughly chopped

3 balls of mozzarella cheese, the best you can get your hands on

To make the dough, sift the flours together and add the salt. Mix the yeast, water and oil together in a bowl. Make a well in the flour, and add the yeast liquid. Gradually work the flour and liquid together to form a dough. Continue to knead for 10 minutes, or until the dough is smooth and elastic. Set it aside to rest for 1 hour, or until doubled in size.

On a floured surface, give the dough a small knead to knock the air out of it. If you are planning to use the dough later, wrap it in clingfilm and place it in the fridge. Beware – it will slowly continue to rise...

To make the sauce for the topping, heat the olive oil in a medium saucepan and cook the onions, garlic and chillies (if using) until soft and translucent. Season with salt and pepper, then add the tomatoes and break them down, using a wooden spoon. Bring to the boil, then lower the heat and simmer for 5 minutes. Add the basil and simmer for a further 2 minutes.

Strain the sauce through a sieve, making sure you get as much through as possible. Return to the stove and simmer until reduced by a quarter. Allow to cool, then refrigerate if not using right away.

When ready to cook your pizza, preheat your oven to as hot as it will go and line a couple of baking sheets with oiled baking paper. Roll the dough out nice and thin, aiming for 2mm, give or take, and place it on the prepared baking sheets. Cover with the tomato sauce, then add as much mozzarella as takes your fancy. Bake for approximately 10–12 minutes, or until the dough is cooked and crisp. Note that this varies from oven to oven, so keep a close eye on it.

Finish with torn basil leaves and freshly ground black pepper.

HERE ARE SOME OF THE VARIATIONS OUR CHEFS EAT...

Lewis – n'duja and Gruyère, with caramelized onions and any chilli that's lying about

Me – sausage, broccoli and smoked scamorza

Francesco – prosciutto with rocket

Daniel B – smoked salmon, poached egg, truffle and hollandaise (trying to bankrupt us)

This is another great dish for snacking at any time – in the afternoon, pre-dinner, or when you get home late at night – and they also go really well with grilled meats, especially in barbecue season. Once cooked, they keep for a few days, so you can just take them out of the fridge and crisp them in the oven, or in a deep-fat fryer if you have one.

Polenta Chips
with Truffled Pecorino Dip

Makes: 18

Preparation time: 10 minutes, plus chilling

Cooking time: 1½ hours

250ml milk

250ml Chicken Stock
(see page 216)

75g onions, finely chopped

1 bay leaf

2 cloves

⅓ nutmeg, grated

125g Instant polenta

100g Parmesan cheese, grated

olive oil or vegetable oil,
for cooking (see method)

1 sprig of fresh rosemary
(optional)

sea salt and freshly ground
black pepper

For the truffled pecorino dip

5 tablespoons Mayonnaise
(see page 217)

100g aged pecorino cheese,
finely grated

20g truffle peelings,
finely chopped

2 leaves of fresh chives,
finely chopped

Put the milk, chicken stock, onions, bay leaf, cloves and nutmeg into a medium saucepan. Bring to just below boiling point, then lower the heat and cook for 30 minutes. Remove the bay leaf and cloves, and add the polenta. Stir well and often, keeping the temperature low enough so that it doesn't splutter too much. Within 8–10 minutes it should be cooked and smooth. Add the Parmesan and mix well.

Turn out on to a baking tray lined with baking paper – it should be big enough to allow the polenta to set 2cm high. Cover the top directly with clingfilm, so it's touching, to prevent a skin from forming, and place in the fridge to set.

When chilled and firm, take the polenta out of the fridge and cut it into chips 2cm wide and approximately 8cm long (or however long you like).

At this stage you can either lightly coat the chips with olive oil, add some rosemary and roast in the oven at 180°C/gas mark 4 for 12 minutes, or until golden. Alternatively, you can deep-fry them for 3 minutes at 170°C until crisp, dropping a sprig of rosemary in there too, to serve alongside the chips and dip.

For the dip, mix all the ingredients together. When the chips are cooked, season with salt and pepper and serve immediately.

These are one of our most successful snacks, in fact one of the most successful dishes we serve. They are great with a cocktail, a beer, as a snack before dinner or at 2 a.m., on the way home, or even instead of dessert.

Barbecue Spiced Pig's Ears

Serves: 6 as a snack

Day 1
Preparation time: 20 minutes
Cooking time: 3 hours

Day 2
Preparation time: 5 minutes
Cooking time: 5 minutes

For the pig's ears
6 pig's ears, washed
1 onion, peeled
2 sticks of celery
2 carrots, peeled
2 bay leaves
1 sprig of fresh thyme
10 peppercorns
vegetable oil, for deep-frying
plain flour, for dusting
sea salt

For the spice mix
60g smoked paprika
20g onion powder
20g garlic powder
40g table salt
60g light brown sugar

DAY 1

Give the ears a good scrub in cold water. Place them in a saucepan and cover them with cold water. Bring to the boil, then pour off the water and transfer the ears to a clean saucepan. Fill with fresh, clean, cold water and add the whole vegetables, herbs and peppercorns. Slowly bring to the boil, skimming constantly. Once at the boil, lower the heat to a simmer and cook for 3 hours.

Allow to cool in the cooking liquid, then lift out and place on a baking tray lined with greaseproof paper. Place another sheet of paper on top, and lay another tray on top of that. Place in the fridge, and put anything heavy you may have on top – this could be a few tins or a couple of plates. Leave overnight.

DAY 2

Heat the oil to 180 °C in your deep-fat fryer or in a deep heavy-based saucepan.

When the ears are cold they will be nice and firm; this makes them much easier to cut. Slice them as thinly as you can, aiming for 1–2mm thick, and dust with flour. Shake off the excess and place in the fryer for 3–4 minutes, or until crisp. Be careful of any spitting fat here, and have a lid or splatter screen ready to slip on top of the fryer once the ears go in.

Keep an eye on the temperature of the oil, as it can sometimes drop when you add the ears. If it does, just tweak it up to 190 °C so it regulates itself.

Remove from the fryer, place on a plate lined with kitchen paper to drain any excess oil, then transfer to a mixing bowl. Mix all the spice mix ingredients together. Add 2 teaspoons of the spice mix to the ears, shake them around until all of them are coated, and add a little sea salt too.

Inspired by the crisps, these pork skin 'quavers' require a long process of dehydration, but once dry they keep for weeks. As well as a snack, they also work really well as a garnish to any pork dish. Instead of buying a sheet of pork skin, you can just trim the skin off any pork you use and freeze it until you have enough to make a batch. You can also use traditional crackling instead, although this will be much richer.

Pork Skin 'Quavers' with Chilli Cream Cheese

Makes: 40

Preparation time: 12 hours, plus cooling

Cooking time: 5 minutes

1 sheet of uncooked pork skin, approximately 45 x 25cm

vegetable oil, for deep-frying

sea salt

For the chilli cream cheese

5 tablespoons cream cheese

1 chipotle en adobo from a jar, ground to a coarse paste

2 sprigs of fresh coriander, chopped

2 sprigs of fresh mint, chopped

Wash the pork skin in cold water, then place in a large saucepan and cover with cold water. Bring to the boil, skimming frequently. Once boiling, pour off the water and cover the skin with fresh cold water. Bring to the boil again, then lower the heat to a gentle simmer. Continue to cook for approximately 1 hour, then remove from the pan to a wire rack and leave to cool.

When cool enough to handle, slice off the layer of fat and any meat still remaining, and then, with a knife blade, continue to scrape as much fat as possible from the skin. Leaving even a little bit behind will stop the skin becoming quaver-like – you need to be left with a sheet of pure skin. Cut into 2.5cm squares, and put on a baking sheet lined with baking paper.

Put the squares in the oven at 70°C/gas mark as low as it will go (try to leave the door open a little) and in 12 hours they should become completely hard and dry like little pieces of brown plastic. It helps to press a piece of kitchen towel on them every couple of hours, to absorb any fat.

When ready to cook, heat the oil to 180°C in a deep-fat fryer or in a deep heavy-based saucepan. Drop in the little pieces of skin, a few at a time, and watch them puff up within a few minutes to five times their size. You may need to flip them over after 2 minutes so they puff up evenly. Don't be worried if nothing happens for the first 20–30 seconds – this is completely normal.

Remove from the fryer or saucepan and place on a plate lined with kitchen paper. Season with salt. Try playing with different flavoured salts, such as chilli or lime.

To make the chilli cream cheese, put the cream cheese in a bowl and mix in the chipotle chilli and chopped herbs. Serve alongside the quavers.

I've always been fascinated with baozi (steamed buns). They are the perfect vehicle for pretty much any slow-cooked meat or even for fish, such as Singapore chilli crab. One day at the restaurant we were playing around with different fillings, and were most satisfied when we tried stuffing them with one of our breakfast components, bacon jam. This was also what made us start playing around with savoury doughnuts...

Bacon Jam Steamed Buns

Makes: 24

Preparation time: 20 minutes, plus proving

Cooking time: 3 hours

For the steamed buns

400g plain flour

60g caster sugar

2 teaspoons / 1 (7g) packet instant dry yeast

1½ teaspoons baking powder

1 teaspoon salt

220ml water

3 tablespoons lard, melted

oil, for greasing

For the bacon jam

500g smoked streaky bacon, cut into small lardons

2 onions, finely chopped

2 garlic cloves, finely chopped

2 tablespoons aji panca, or chipotle en adobo from a jar

½ teaspoon smoked paprika

3 tablespoons brown sugar

3 tablespoons black treacle

75ml cider vinegar

2 shots espresso

You will also need a steamer

To make the bacon jam, put the bacon into a frying pan over a low heat and cook slowly to render the fat. As the fat melts, pour it away so you have just the meat left. Keep cooking until the bacon starts to caramelize. The brown bits that stick to the bottom are all good, so scrape them off and leave them in the frying pan.

Add the onions and garlic, and continue to cook, with no colour, until soft. Add the aji panca, smoked paprika and brown sugar and cook for a further 5 minutes. Add the treacle, vinegar and espresso and simmer gently until the mixture has a jam-like consistency. This should take an hour or so. Place into a sterilized container, allow to cool, then cover and refrigerate.

To make the buns, sift the flour into a bowl and mix in the sugar, yeast, baking powder and salt. Mix the water and lard together, then add to the flour and blend together. Knead for 10 minutes by hand. Place in a clean bowl, cover with a tea towel and set aside to prove until doubled in size – 40 minutes should do.

Knock the air out of the dough and divide it into 24 golfball-size pieces. Let them rest for 5 minutes. Flatten each one into a disc and place a teaspoon of bacon jam inside, then bring up the sides of the dough and seal into a ball. Place each ball on an individual piece of well-oiled baking paper, then set aside to prove for 20 minutes.

Place each ball on its paper inside a steamer, 4 at a time. Steam for approximately 12–15 minutes and serve immediately.

By **Richard Woods**,
Head of Spirit and Cocktail Development
at Samba Brands Management

COCKTAILS

I was first introduced to the hospitality industry in 1999, when a new 'gastro' bar near my home was looking for bartenders and servers – I still have the recipe cards for the small cocktail list that we were told to learn before we opened. Looking back now, I would say that this point marked the beginning of my hospitality career. A few years later in 2007, and after a move to London, I was heading up the bar at Floridita in London, taking over from legendary bartender Nick Strangeway. This became my introduction to the London bar scene and also to cocktails, and during my time there I continued to learn about spirits, drinks, history and trends. I visited different cities, both in the UK and abroad, taking notes on my findings for a serve or ideas for flavour pairings.

Since joining Samba Brands Management in 2012, I have worked to create what I refer to as an iconoclastic bar and menu, to illustrate my desire to show how drinking is an experience. I play with flavour pairings and savoury elements to show how flavour is as much about aroma as taste – actually, it's more about aroma as taste. It's also about bridging the gap between food and drink to encapsulate a complete dining experience. You may describe my drinks as weird and quirky, but thought goes into every serve. I take inspiration from all manner of resources: a dinner out, a memorable day, a time of the year or a personal feeling. I often ask, how can I make a drink better, lighter, fresher or more flavourful? The following recipes are some that I created prior to Duck & Waffle, some that we have served since opening and others that are entirely new.

Like many of the drinks in this chapter, the JD & C requires a bit of preparation, in this instance making the cola reduction. The recipe below is for making the cocktail at home and differs slightly from the one we follow in the bar. Among other things, we have chosen here to substitute a more readily available vanilla pod for the very aromatic tonka bean that we usually use. (For a simpler version, you can use cola syrup for a SodaStream and add it directly to the drink.)

JD & C

Serves: 1

Preparation time: 45 minutes

Glass: stemless wine glass/ rocks glass

50ml Jack Daniels

4 teaspoons salted cola reduction (see below)

1 teaspoon Aperol

1 teaspoon white cacao liqueur

a dash of Angostura bitters

a dash of cider vinegar

ice cubes, to stir and serve

For the salted cola reduction
(makes enough for 5 cocktails)

330ml flat cola

10g caster sugar

¼ teaspoon sea salt

½ a vanilla pod

To make the salted cola reduction, put the cola into a saucepan over a high heat and let it bubble away until it has reduced to one-third of its original volume. Add the sugar, salt and half vanilla pod, and cook for a further 20 minutes, stirring. Allow to cool, then strain into a glass jar or non-reactive container and reserve.

To make your JD&C, stir all the ingredients together with ice cubes and strain into a glass over fresh ice.

Serves: 1
Preparation time: 15 minutes
Glass: chilled champagne flute

For the Bellini
50ml celery mix (see below)
75ml prosecco

For the celery mix
(makes enough for 5 cocktails)
140ml celery juice
30ml cucumber juice
75ml cloudy apple juice
20ml sugar syrup
1 teaspoon wasabi paste

This take on a Bellini started life as a completely different cocktail. I first began experimenting with celery in a drink called Astoria, named after the Waldorf Astoria's signature salad – celery, walnuts and blue cheese (yep)! Looking for something to lift the lighter notes of the celery, I played around with more robust, earthy tastes and found that wasabi worked really well. The blue cheese was dropped and I ended up with a celery and wasabi Bellini – earthy, fresh and slightly floral.

Celery and Wasabi Bellini

To make the celery mix, combine the celery, cucumber and apple juices in a jug or bowl and stir in the sugar syrup and wasabi. Pass through a sieve to get rid of any unwanted fibres, then pour into a glass jar or non-reactive container, put the lid on, and reserve. The mix will keep in the fridge for up to 2 days and will retain its bright colour. As soon as it starts to look dull, discard.

Put the celery mix into a chilled champagne flute, top up with Prosecco and stir gently.

Serves: 1
Preparation time: 2 days
Glass: stemless wine glass/ rocks glass

1 egg white
2 teaspoons truffle oil
25ml fresh lemon juice
20ml sugar syrup
60ml rosemary-infused whisky (see below)
ice cubes, to stir and serve

For the rosemary-infused whisky
300ml whisky
2 or 3 sprigs of fresh rosemary

I love egg white in cocktails. It's a great binder, allowing you to mix and hold all the flavours and add texture. With this sour, I wanted a rich earthiness that would marry well with whisky. I played around with the flavour of truffle, but it was too overpowering, so I found a way to deliver the aroma of truffle without too much of the flavour – a truffle foam. It was one of the first drinks on Duck & Waffle's cocktail menu and we still make it today.

Truffle Sour

To make the rosemary-infused whisky, put the whisky into a glass jar or non-reactive container with the rosemary sprigs and leave to infuse for 48 hours.

In the bar we use a whipping canister to make truffle foam, but this simpler all-in-one version also works well. Place the egg white in a shaker, and add the truffle oil, lemon juice and sugar syrup. Shake vigorously for approximately 1 minute. Don't add any ice at this stage. You are looking for a creamy, fluffy texture.

Add the rosemary-infused whisky to the shaker. Fill with ice and shake again, then strain into a glass over fresh ice.

I first visited New York in 2004, and I found the pairing of bacon and maple syrup that they use there both weird and totally moreish. A few years later when I was developing my bartending skills and palate, I remembered this combination of savoury and sweet, and the first drink I adapted using this pairing was an Old Fashioned. This has since developed further into the Bacon and Salted Caramel Manhattan.

Bacon and Salted Caramel Manhattan

Serves: 1

Preparation time: 3½ hours

Glass: chilled Martini/ coupette glass

65ml bacon-infused Bourbon (see below)

25ml Martini Rosso (sweet vermouth)

15ml salted caramel liqueur (see below)

5ml sugar syrup

2 dashes of Angostura bitters

ice cubes, to stir

For the bacon infused Bourbon
(makes enough for 5 cocktails)

8 rashers of smoky bacon

350ml Bourbon (Woodford Reserve works best)

For the salted caramel liqueur
(makes enough for 5 cocktails)

30g caster sugar

10ml water

1 teaspoon salt

100ml neutral grain spirit (a vodka at 40% abv works well)

You will also need a large ziplock freezer bag and a sugar thermometer

To make the bacon-infused Bourbon, cook the bacon in a frying pan until crisp. Once cooked, turn off the heat and let the bacon rest for a few minutes.

Meanwhile, prepare your homemade water bath. Pour water two-thirds of the way up the sides of a deep saucepan or wok (better) and place over a medium heat. Do not let the water boil, as this will damage the quality of the alcohol (you want it at a constant 60°C).

Pour the Bourbon into a large ziplock freezer bag and add the bacon (complete with any fat and juices). Seal the bag, removing as much air as possible and making sure you don't tear it. Put the bag into your water bath and leave for 55 minutes, then remove and place on a tea towel to dry. Transfer the mix to a non-reactive container, seal and place in the freezer for 2 hours.

When you take it out of the freezer you will notice that the freezing process has made the bacon fat separate and solidify, allowing the alcohol to be filtered off cleanly and clearly. Line a funnel or sieve with two-fold muslin (a coffee filter or tea towel works well too) and put it over an empty glass jar or deep container. Remove the bacon pieces, then strain the liquid through the muslin – this process will take up to 30 minutes. When ready, put a lid on and reserve.

To make the salted caramel liqueur, put the sugar into a large saucepan over a high heat. Allow the sugar to brown and caramelize, then add the water and salt, stirring all the time. Once the sugar has burnt and turned to a treacle-like liquid, remove the pan from the heat and add the grain spirit, stirring constantly to prevent the caramel solidifying. Allow to cool.

Line a funnel or sieve with two-fold muslin (or a coffee filter or tea towel) and put it over an empty glass jar or deep container. Strain the caramel liquid through the muslin to catch any bits of solidified caramel – this will only take a few minutes. When ready, put a lid on and reserve.

To make your Manhattan, combine all the ingredients in a mixing glass with ice cubes and stir until icy cold, then strain into a chilled glass.

Serves: 1

Preparation time: 5 minutes

Glass: chilled Martini/
coupette glass

1 lemon wedge

25ml gin (45% or higher – Plymouth Navy strength works well)

50ml Martini Rosso
(sweet vermouth)

2 bar spoons maraschino liqueur

3 drops of orange bitters
(Fee Brothers or Regan's)

1 bar spoon sugar syrup

ice cubes, to stir

The Martinez is by far the simplest cocktail in this book, and shows that elegant and flavourful cocktails can also be simple. Recently I've played with adding a chocolate flavour, which works great alongside the orange notes of the bitters. When chilled enough, it tastes a bit like a Jaffa cake. But I've also experimented with bitters, essence and a house-made liqueur. Wow! What a combination. The citrus works so well with gin and adds to the vermouth's lift.

Martinez

Squeeze the juice from the lemon wedge directly into a mixing glass or cocktail shaker. Add the remaining ingredients and ice cubes and stir until icy cold, then strain into a chilled glass.

Serves: 1

Preparation time: 1 day

Glass: chilled Martini/
coupette glass

65ml vodka (Grey Goose works best)

15ml dry vermouth

60ml Bloody Mary consommé
(see below)

ice cubes, to stir

For the Bloody Mary consommé
(makes enough for 5 cocktails)

400ml good-quality tomato juice

3g ground black pepper

5g crushed pink peppercorns

3g sea salt

2g celery salt

1 teaspoon Tabasco

1¼ teaspoons Green Tabasco

juice of 1 lemon

3 teaspoons Worcestershire sauce

A Bloody Mary makes a great cocktail. It can be quite filling though, so I decided to play with its texture, thinning the juice while retaining the flavour. Eventually I achieved a kind of Bloody Mary consommé which, instead of being served long, was strong enough in flavour to be used in small amounts with vodka, gin or vermouth to make a Martini. Essentially this drink is all in the preparation. Freeze a batch of the Bloody Mary consommé and simply allow it to defrost through muslin or a clean tea towel – the end result is amazingly rich yet lightly textured.

Essence of Mary

To make the Bloody Mary consommé, pour the tomato juice into a non-reactive container. Add the other ingredients and stir, then leave to rest for 30 minutes. Put a lid on the container and place in the freezer overnight.

The following morning, line a funnel or sieve with two-fold muslin (a coffee filter or tea towel works well too) and put it on top of an empty glass jar or deep container. Strain the frozen tomato mix through the muslin, allowing it to drip and thaw naturally (this takes several hours). When ready, put a lid on and reserve.

To make your Essence of Mary, combine all the ingredients in a mixing glass or cocktail shaker with ice cubes and stir, then strain into a chilled glass. Garnish as you wish – try a small dehydrated tomato slice.

I started giving my cocktail menus a savory slant back in 2007, and among the results was a roasted sour: seasoned bone marrow cooked with whisky, then drip-thawed to separate liquid and fat, producing a flavourful spirit without any oiliness. Fast-forward four years, and on the very first Duck & Waffle menu the bone marrow seasoning was used in a Cosmopolitan. The combination came about through the idea of a Sunday roast, pairing its savouriness and meatiness with the sweetness of an accompanying preserve such as cranberry. It really works.

Roast Cosmo

Serves: 1

Preparation time: 3 hours

Glass: chilled Martini/coupette glass

50ml roast cosmo mix (see below)

35ml cranberry juice

1 teaspoon lime juice

1 teaspoon lime cordial

1 teaspoon white cacao liqueur

lime wedge or zest, to garnish

ice cubes, to stir

For the roast cosmo mix
(makes enough for 5 cocktails)

2 pieces of bone marrow

sea salt and freshly ground black pepper

2 sprigs of fresh rosemary

175ml Grey Goose Le Citron vodka

75ml Triple Sec, or other good-quality orange liqueur

You will also need a large ziplock freezer bag and a sugar thermometer

To make the roast cosmo mix, preheat your oven to 200 °C/gas mark 6. Put the bone marrow on a baking tray, season with salt and pepper and add a couple of rosemary sprigs. Cook in the oven for 20–25 minutes, or until the marrow is cooked through. Remove from the oven and let it rest for a few minutes.

Meanwhile, prepare your homemade water bath. Pour water two-thirds of the way up the sides of a deep saucepan or wok (better) and place over a medium heat. Do not let the water boil, as this will damage the quality of the alcohol (you want it at a constant 60 °C).

Put the vodka and Triple Sec into a large ziplock freezer bag and add the roasted bone marrow complete with the herbs and any juices. Seal the bag, removing as much air as possible and making sure no sharp pieces of bone can tear it. Put the bag into your water bath and leave for 45 minutes, then remove and place on a tea towel to dry. Transfer the mix to a non-reactive container, seal and place in the freezer for 2 hours.

When you take it out of the freezer you will notice that the freezing process has made the bone marrow fat separate and solidify, allowing the alcohol to be filtered off cleanly and clearly. Line a funnel or sieve with two-fold muslin (a coffee filter or tea towel works well too) and put it on top of an empty glass jar or deep container. Remove the marrow pieces first, then strain the liquid through the muslin – this process will take up to 30 minutes. When ready, put a lid on and reserve.

To make your Roast Cosmo, shake all the ingredients except the garnish with ice cubes and double strain into a chilled glass. Garnish with a lime wedge or zest.

Left to right: Cereal Killer Old Fashioned, Prairie Provençal, Roast Cosmo

This one is for the kids among us. Chocolate rice pops is such a great cereal – malty, chocolatey – and for me, a bowlful with some ice-cold milk still brings back happy childhood memories. You can capture this nostalgic flavour by adding the cereal to a glass of Bourbon. I investigated various cereals but found that my favourite worked best. The only problem I've encountered is that I find my days are a lot slower if I start the morning with more than one of these!

Cereal Killer Old Fashioned

Serves: 1

Preparation time: 3½ hours–3 days

Glass: large rocks glass

65ml chocolate rice pop-infused Bourbon (see below)

10ml sugar syrup

2 dashes of Angostura bitters

ice cubes, to stir and serve

For the chocolate rice pop-infused Bourbon
(makes enough for 5 cocktails)

400g chocolate-flavoured rice pop cereal

400ml Bourbon (Woodford Reserve works best)

You will also need a large ziplock freezer bag and a sugar thermometer

In the bar we use the sous-vide method to make the infused Bourbon, but there are two alternative methods that I have found work well at home. The first is the lazy approach and requires more infusing time. The second is quicker but requires more attention. Note: The reason for the higher volume of alcohol used in this recipe is due to the absorption of the chocolate-flavoured rice cereal. Once you strain off the liquid, you will find that you lose up to 15 per cent.

METHOD 1
Put the cereal into a glass jar or non-reactive container and cover with the Bourbon. Put the lid on and leave for a minimum of 72 hours, or until you are happy with the results, periodically tasting (remember to gently shake the jar or container every now and again, to release more flavour). Once you are happy with your infusion, line a funnel or sieve with two-fold muslin (a coffee filter or tea towel works well too) and put it on top of an empty glass jar or deep container. Strain the mix through the muslin. When ready, put a lid on and reserve.

METHOD 2
Meanwhile, prepare your homemade water bath. Pour water two-thirds of the way up the sides of a deep saucepan or wok (better) and place over a medium heat. Do not let the water boil, as this will damage the quality of the alcohol (you want it at a constant 60°C).

Put the bourbon and cereal into a large ziplock freezer bag and seal, removing as much air as possible and being careful not to tear the bag. Put the bag into your water bath and leave for 1 hour, then remove and place on a tea towel to cool. Transfer the mix to a non-reactive container, seal and place in the freezer for 2 hours.

When you take it out, you will notice that the freezing process has made the cereal solidify, allowing the alcohol to be filtered off cleanly and clearly. Line a funnel or sieve with two-fold muslin (a coffee filter or tea towel works well too) and put it on top of an empty glass jar or deep container. Strain the liquid through the muslin – this process will take up to 30 minutes. When ready, put a lid on and reserve.

To make your Cereal Killer Old Fashioned, combine all the ingredients in a mixing glass with ice cubes and stir until icy cold, then strain into an iced-filled rocks glass.

Serves: 1

Preparation time: 5 minutes

Glass: chilled small tasting glass or liqueur glass

1 duck egg yolk

50ml Bombay Sapphire gin

2 teaspoons tomato ketchup

25ml tomato juice

a pinch of salt

a pinch of black pepper

a dash of balsamic vinegar

micro coriander leaves, to garnish (optional)

ice cubes, to stir

When creating a drink, it's important to think about why you are doing it – it might be meant as a drink to have on its own, or it might be intended to accompany food, without taking away from the food itself. This little cocktail was created for sipping with oysters. It's powerful and strong, so you only need to serve it in small tasting measures. The sharpness of the ketchup and the calmness of the coriander work well with the gin.

Prairie Provençal

Place the yolk in the bottom of your glass.

Shake the remaining ingredients, apart from the micro coriander, with ice cubes and double strain into your glass, on top of the yolk. Garnish with micro coriander leaves, if you like.

This cocktail is inspired by the most quintessential flavours of the sea and is one of the best pairings.

Perle de Mer

Serves: 1

Preparation time: 1 day

Glass: chilled Martini glass

50ml Grey Goose vodka

25ml 'sea spray' vermouth (see below)

1 teaspoon olive jus

ice cubes, to stir and serve

1 caper berry, to garnish

For the 'sea spray' vermouth
(makes enough for 5 cocktails)

125ml Noilly Prat vermouth

1 freshly shucked oyster shell

To make the 'sea spray' vermouth, put the Noilly Prat into a non-reactive container and add the oyster shell. Leave overnight to infuse.

The following morning, line a funnel or sieve with two-fold muslin (a coffee filter or tea towel works well too) and set it on top of an empty jar or non-reactive container. Discard the oyster shell and strain the vermouth through the muslin.

To make your Perle de Mer, combine all the ingredients in a mixing glass with ice cubes and stir until icy cold, then strain into a chilled glass and garnish with a caper berry.

RECIPE BASICS

CHICKEN STOCK

Makes: 1 litre

3 chicken carcasses
1 onion, peeled and halved
1 stick of celery
1 leek, halved
1 bay leaf
10 black peppercorns
1 sprig of fresh thyme

Place all the ingredients in a large saucepan, leaving the vegetables in whole pieces (halves where stated) so that they don't break down as the stock cooks. Cover with cold water, then slowly bring to the boil, skimming off any fat or foam as they arise. Lower the heat and simmer for 3 hours. The more fat and impurities you manage to remove, the clearer, and therefore purer, your stock will be.

At the end of the 3 hours, strain the stock through a sieve lined with a fine cloth, by slowly pouring it through – don't press anything or it will become cloudy. Pour into a clean saucepan and simmer until reduced by half. Strain again and chill.

BRINE

Makes: 1 litre

1 litre water
50g sea salt
20 peppercorns
2 bay leaves
5 juniper berries
20 coriander seeds

Bring the water to the boil in a large saucepan, then turn the heat off. Add the salt, let it dissolve, then add the rest of the ingredients and allow to cool.

When cold, the brine is ready to use.

PICKLING LIQUID

Makes: 300ml

200ml white wine vinegar
100ml water
80g caster sugar
10g salt
a pinch of coriander seeds
a pinch of black peppercorns
1 bay leaf

Put all the ingredients into a large saucepan and bring to the boil, then strain and allow to cool.

To use, put whatever ingredients you want to pickle into sterilized jars, pour over the pickling liquid and seal the jars tightly. Leave to pickle for a minimum of 1 day and up to 1 week.

SHERRY DRESSING

Serves: 2–3

50ml olive oil
50ml sherry vinegar

Put the olive oil and sherry vinegar into a bowl and whisk together. Don't worry if it separates when you set it aside – just give it a stir before you need to use it.

BALSAMIC GLAZE

Makes: approximately 200ml

500ml good-quality
balsamic vinegar

Put the vinegar into a saucepan over a medium heat and simmer until it has reduced by half and has a honey-like consistency. Be careful, as it goes from honey to burnt in seconds. This should take around 20 minutes.

Towards the end, give the vinegar a swirl or a stir every couple of minutes, as this is when the sugars begin to thicken and it may start to catch on the bottom of the pan.

CONFIT SHALLOTS

Makes: approximately 100g

300ml olive oil
pinch of salt
5 banana shallots, finely diced

Put the oil, salt and shallots into a saucepan and heat gently for 30 minutes, or until the shallots are soft with no colour. This will keep, covered with the oil, for up to a week.

CONFIT GARLIC

Makes: approximately 18 cloves

3 heads of garlic, broken into
cloves (not peeled)
300ml olive oil

Put the garlic cloves into a saucepan, cover with the olive oil, and heat gently for 30 minutes, or until the garlic is soft. Be careful not to let it colour.

Store the cloves in the oil, which is great to use on its own, on pizza or salads.

MAYONNAISE

Makes: 400ml

2 egg yolks
1 tablespoon Dijon mustard
50ml white wine vinegar
400ml groundnut oil
sea salt and freshly ground
white pepper

In a food processor, whisk the egg yolks, mustard and vinegar together. Slowly start adding the oil, and if the mix doesn't continue to blend together, slow the machine down a little. If the mix becomes too thick and excessively greasy, add warm water, a teaspoonful at a time, until it loosens up a bit. Season with salt and white pepper.

DUCK CURE

Makes: 350g

180g salt
180g caster sugar
5g orange zest
a pinch of ground cinnamon
1 clove
1 star anise
5 pink peppercorns
20ml brandy

Mix all the ingredients together and store in an airtight container.

STANDARD CURE

Makes: 80g

50g sea salt
25g sugar
2 sprigs of fresh thyme, leaves picked
10 black peppercorns
1 star anise

Mix all the ingredients together and store in an airtight container.

GRANOLA

This makes quite a lot, and it's a great ingredient to have in your cupboard. You can easily halve the ingredients if you want to make a smaller amount.

Makes: 1kg

500g oats
100g hazelnuts
100g almonds
100g pistachios
100g pecan nuts
25g sesame seeds
25g sunflower seeds
25g pumpkin seeds
125g golden syrup
100g honey
125g raisins
125g dried apricots

Preheat your oven to 160°C/gas mark 3.

Put all the ingredients except the dried fruit into a bowl and mix together well. Divide between 2 large lipped baking sheets lined with baking paper. Bake in the oven for 40 minutes, giving a mix every 10 minutes so it all becomes evenly coloured.

Remove from the oven, mix in the dried fruit and allow to cool.

HONEYCOMB

When adding the bicarbonate of soda, do be aware that it rises and expands very quickly – be ready!

Makes: 1 medium tray

50g honey
70ml water
125g glucose
325g caster sugar
25g bicarbonate of soda

You will also need a sugar thermometer

Line a deep roasting tray with baking paper.

Put all the ingredients except for the bicarbonate of soda into a large saucepan over a medium heat. Allow the sugar to dissolve, then continue to cook until a temperature of 155°C is reached on a sugar thermometer.

Remove from the heat and add the bicarbonate of soda. Whisk well, then pour into the prepared tray. Allow to cool and set.

When cool and firm, smash the honeycomb into smaller pieces. Store in an airtight container for up to 2–3 weeks.

VANILLA ICE CREAM

Makes: 1 litre

500ml milk
500ml double cream
seeds from 1 vanilla pod
190g caster sugar
10 egg yolks

Bring the milk, cream and vanilla to the boil in a large saucepan. Meanwhile, put the sugar and egg yolks into a bowl and whisk very well. (Sugar absorbs moisture, and if you don't mix straight away you will have pieces of dried egg yolk where all the moisture has been removed by the sugar, so beware.)

Once the milk and cream comes to the boil, pour half on to the yolk mix and whisk together. Pour this back into the remaining milk and cream in the saucepan and heat gently until thickened. In the kitchen we use a thermometer to check once it is cooked (84°C is the temperature we take it to – any higher and the egg will scramble, leaving your ice cream lumpy), but if you don't have one, cook until it coats the back of a wooden spoon and stays there without running off straight away. Strain the mixture, transfer to another bowl to stop it cooking, then cool and churn.

If you don't have an ice cream machine, freeze the mixture in four batches and, once frozen, blend in a food processor. Return to the freezer after blending.

INDEX

AUTHOR'S ACKNOWLEDGEMENTS

This page is often the last piece of text to be written, which seems wrong, but, having seen the sheer amount of work that goes into writing a book, and all the wonderful people involved, I now appreciate how many people I would have missed, and I'm glad that I am able to thank everyone who has made this happen.

I don't have the talents to write a speech, nor enough ways to say, 'I'd like to thank…' and, as a life-long list-writer, I'm going to list it out and pray I haven't forgotten anyone.

Maureen Mills, for introducing me to the wonderful Alison Starling, who, between them, made this dream come true and have guided me at every stage.

Samba Brands Management, for giving me this opportunity to fulfil my dream and for letting me do it my way.

Everyone at Octopus Publishing, especially Sybella, Juliette & Katherine for sharing their expertise.

Anders Schønnemann. He's the guy who took the photos that took my breath away, a huge talent and a great man who we were very lucky to have, and his 'always hungry' assistant Louise.

Annie Rigg, for making my recipes look fantastic. I cannot portray how impressed I was with not only her supreme level of cooking, but the eye for food styling. Another level, and I'd give her any job in my kitchen.

Kat Mead, recipe tester extraordinaire. She helped translate chef speak into normal comprehensible English, which is no easy task, let me tell you.

All of our suppliers for helping out, including Simpsons, Rhug Estate, Parsley in Time, Flour Station and Nisbets.

Billingsgate Market, for allowing us to get messy taking pictures of fish.

The kitchen team at the restaurant, led by Tom Cenci, my best friend and life-saver – nothing would have been possible without his support. I am forever in his debt for how he has helped me at D&W. Jacek, Kamil, Francesco, Janos & Daniel, together with Tomek, Chris, Michael, David W, Manny, Seb, Jon, Billy, Lewis, Ewa, Tammy, Borja, Junior, Luca, Suza, Pedro, Matt, Yamil, Andrea, Jorge, David A, and Rafael, thank you all guys.

Thanks to Chan and Richard for their expertise on the desserts and drinks respectively.

All of our guests and friends on social media for being so supportive, whether telling us what you love, or even what you don't. That's the only way we learn and thank you for being so honest.

And last, but not least, I'd like to thank Marcella, my beautiful wife. Being a chef's wife is a huge sacrifice, one that she never complains about. She has shown nothing but support for my career during the 10 years we have known each other, and I am incredibly lucky to have her in my life. That is something I will never forget. Thank you thank you thank you.